HOUGHTON MIFFLIN   BOSTON

Program Authors

William Badders
Director of the Cleveland Mathematics
and Science Partnership
Cleveland Municipal School District
Cleveland, Ohio

Douglas Carnine, Ph.D.
Professor of Education
University of Oregon
Eugene, Oregon

James Feliciani
Supervisor of Instructional
Media and Technology
Land O' Lakes, Florida

Bobby Jeanpierre, Ph.D.
Assistant Professor, Science Education
University of Central Florida
Orlando, Florida

Carolyn Sumners, Ph.D.
Director of Astronomy and Physical Sciences
Houston Museum of Natural Science
Houston, Texas

Catherine Valentino
Author-in-Residence
Houghton Mifflin
West Kingston, Rhode Island

Content Consultants

Dr. Robert Arnold
Professor of Biology
Colgate University
Hamilton, New York

Dr. Carl D. Barrentine
Associate Professor of Humanities
and Biology
University of North Dakota
Grand Forks, North Dakota

Dr. Steven L. Bernasek
Department of Chemistry
Princeton University
Princeton, New Jersey

Dennis W. Cheek
Senior Manager
Science Applications International
Corporation
Exton, Pennsylvania

Dr. Jung Choi
School of Biology
Georgia Tech
Atlanta, Georgia

Prof. John Conway
Department of Physics
University of California
Davis, California

Copyright © 2007 by Houghton Mifflin Company. All rights reserved.

No part of this work may be reproduced or transmitted in any form or by any means, electronic or mechanical, including photocopying or recording, or by any information storage or retrieval system without prior written permission of Houghton Mifflin Company unless such copying is expressly permitted by federal copyright law. Address inquiries to School Permissions, 222 Berkeley St., Boston, MA 02116.

Printed in the U.S.A.

ISBN-13: 978-0-618-62463-8
ISBN-10: 0-618-62463-5

2 3 4 5 6 7 8 9-DW-14 13 12 11 10 09 08 07

Content Consultants

Dr. Robert Dailey
Division of Animal and Veterinary Sciences
West Virginia University
Morgantown, West Virginia

Dr. Thomas Davies
IODP/USIO Science Services
Texas A & M University
College Station, Texas

Dr. Ron Dubreuil
Department of Biological Sciences
University of Illinois at Chicago
Chicago, Illinois

Dr. Orin G. Gelderloos
Professor of Biology
University of Michigan - Dearborn
Dearborn, Michigan

Dr. Michael R. Geller
Associate Professor, Department of Physics
University of Georgia
Athens, Georgia

Dr. Erika Gibb
Department of Physics
Notre Dame University
South Bend, Indiana

Dr. Fern Gotfried
Pediatrician
Hanover Township, New Jersey

Dr. Michael Haaf
Chemistry Department
Ithaca College
Ithaca, New York

Professor Melissa A. Hines
Department of Chemistry
Cornell University
Ithaca, New York

Dr. Jonathan M. Lincoln
Assistant Provost & Dean of Undergraduate Education
Bloomsburg University
Bloomsburg, Pennsylvania

Donald Lisowy
Wildlife Conservation Society
Bronx Zoo
Bronx, New York

Dr. Marc L. Mansfield
Department of Chemistry and Chemical Biology
Stevens Institute of Technology
Hoboken, New Jersey

Dr. Scott Nuismer
Department of Biological Sciences
University of Idaho
Moscow, Idaho

Dr. Suzanne O'Connell
Department of Earth and Environmental Sciences
Wesleyan University
Middletown, Connecticut

Dr. Kenneth Parsons
Assistant Professor of Meteorology
Embry-Riddle Aeronautical University
Prescott, Arizona

Betty Preece
Engineer and Physicist
Indialantic, Florida

Dr. Chantal Reid
Department of Biology
Duke University
Durham, North Carolina

Dr. Todd V. Royer
Department of Biological Sciences
Kent State University
Kent, Ohio

Dr. Kate Scholberg
Physics Department
Duke University
Durham, North Carolina

Dr. Jeffery Scott
Department of Earth, Atmospheric, and Planetary Sciences
Massachusetts Institute of Technology
Cambridge, Massachusetts

Dr. Ron Stoner
Professor Emeritus, Physics and Astronomy Department
Bowling Green State University
Bowling Green, Ohio

Dr. Dominic Valentino, Ph.D.
Professor, Department of Psychology
University of Rhode Island
Kingston, Rhode Island

Dr. Sidney White
Professor Emeritus of Geology
Ohio State University
Columbus, Ohio

Dr. Scott Wissink
Professor, Department of Physics
Indiana University
Bloomington, Indiana

Dr. David Wright
Department of Chemistry
Vanderbilt University
Nashville, Tennessee

Contents

UNIT A — Plants, Animals, and People

	Reading in Science	A2
Chapter 1	**Plants**	A4
	Lesson 1	A6
	Lesson 2	A12
	Focus On: Technology	A18
	Lesson 3	A20
	Review and SAT 10 Practice	A26
Chapter 2	**Animals**	A28
	Lesson 1	A30
	Focus On: Literature	A36
	Lesson 2	A38
	Lesson 3	A44
	Review and SAT 10 Practice	A50
Chapter 3	**People**	A52
	Lesson 1	A54
	Focus On: Health and Safety	A60
	Lesson 2	A62
	Review and SAT 10 Practice	A70
	Unit A Wrap-Up	A72

UNIT B — Living Things and Where They Live

	Reading in Science B2
Chapter 4	**Living Things** B4
	Lesson 1 . . . . B6
	Focus On: Readers' Theater B12
	Lesson 2 . . . . B14
	Review and SAT 10 Practice B22
Chapter 5	**Where Plants and Animals Live** B24
	Lesson 1 . . . . B26
	Lesson 2 . . . . B32
	Focus On: Biography B38
	Lesson 3 . . . . B40
	Review and SAT 10 Practice B46
	Unit B Wrap-Up B48

v

Contents

Earth, Our Home

	Reading in Science	C2
Chapter 6	**Looking at Our Earth**	C4
	Lesson 1	C6
	Lesson 2	C12
	Focus On: Readers' Theater	C18
	Lesson 3	C22
	Review and SAT 10 Practice	C28
Chapter 7	**Caring for Our Earth**	C30
	Lesson 1	C32
	Lesson 2	C38
	Focus On: Health and Safety	C44
	Lesson 3	C46
	Review and SAT 10 Practice	C54
	Unit C Wrap-Up	C56

UNIT D: Weather and the Sky

Reading in Science	D2
Chapter 8 — Weather and Seasons	D4
Lesson 1	D6
Lesson 2	D12
Focus On: Literature	D18
Lesson 3	D20
Lesson 4	D26
Lesson 5	D32
Review and SAT 10 Practice	D40
Chapter 9 — Changes in the Sky	D42
Lesson 1	D44
Lesson 2	D50
Lesson 3	D56
Focus On: Biography	D62
Lesson 4	D64
Review and SAT 10 Practice	D70
Unit D Wrap-Up	D72

Contents

UNIT E — Describing Matter

	Reading in Science	E2
Chapter 10	**Observing Objects**	E4
	Lesson 1	E6
	Lesson 2	E12
	Lesson 3	E18
	Focus On: Technology	E24
	Lesson 4	E26
	Review and SAT 10 Practice	E32
Chapter 11	**Changes in Matter**	E34
	Lesson 1	E36
	Lesson 2	E42
	Focus On: Literature	E47
	Lesson 3	E48
	Review and SAT 10 Practice	E54
	Unit E Wrap-Up	E56

UNIT F — Energy Sources and Motion

	Reading in Science	F2
Chapter 12	**Heat, Light, and Sound**	F4
	Lesson 1	F6
	Lesson 2	F12
	Lesson 3	F18
	Focus On: Technology	F23
	Lesson 4	F24
	Review and SAT 10 Practice	F30
Chapter 13	**Moving Faster and Slower**	F32
	Lesson 1	F34
	Lesson 2	F40
	Focus On: Readers' Theater	F46
	Lesson 3	F48
	Review and SAT 10 Practice	F54
	Unit F Wrap-Up	F56

ix

Features

UNIT A

Investigate Activities
Observe a Plant A7
Compare Leaves A13
Use Plant Models A21
Hidden Animals A31
Classify Animals A39
A Cat's Life Cycle A45
Model Your Body A55
A Person's Life A63

Reading in Science
What's Alive? by Kathleen Weidner Zoehfeld A2

Focus On
Technology: Plant Power! A18
Literature: "In a Winter Meadow"; *Animal Disguises* A36
Health and Safety: Be Active . . A60

UNIT B

Investigate Activities
Classify Objects B7
Observe Plants B15
Observe a Tree B27
Compare Animals B33
Wet or Dry B41

Reading in Science
Over in the Meadow by Ezra Jack Keats B2

Focus On
Readers' Theater: Living or Nonliving? B12
Biography: Marjory Stoneman Douglas B38

UNIT C

Investigate Activities
Land and Water C7
Compare Rocks C13
Observe Soil C23
Collect Pollution C33
A Waterwheel C39
Sort Your Trash C47

Reading in Science
Dirt by Steve Tomecek C2

Focus On
Readers' Theater: Rock Stars . . C18
Health and Safety: Water Safety C44

UNIT D

Investigate Activities
Record Weather D7
Measure Weather D13
Water Changes D21
Grow Plants D27
What to Wear D33
Observe the Sky D45
Day and Night D51
Moon Changes D57
Sun Changes D65

Reading in Science
What Will the Weather Be?
 by Lynda DeWitt D2

Focus On
Literature: *Rain;* "City Rain" . . . D18
Biography: Galileo Galilei D62

UNIT E

Investigate Activities
Classify Objects E7
Use Tools E13
Use Magnets E19
Float or Sink E27
Compare Matter E37
Predict Changes E43
Make a Mixture E49

Reading in Science
What Is the World Made Of?
 by Kathleen Weidner
 Zoehfeld E2

Focus On
Technology: Mighty Magnets . . E24
Literature: "Ice Cycle" E47

UNIT F

Investigate Activities
Measure Heat F7
Shine Light F13
Make Sounds F19
Different Sounds F25
How Things Move F35
Compare Distance F41
Change Motion F49

Reading in Science
Energy: Heat, Light, and Fuel
 by Darlene Stille F2

Focus On
Technology: Thump, Thump! . . . F23
Readers' Theater: Fast Rides
 and Slow Lines F46

About Your Textbook

How Your Book Is Organized

The Nature of Science

In the front of your book you will learn about how people explore science.

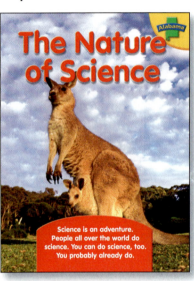

Units

The major sections of your book are units.

Unit Title tells you what the unit is about.

Find more information related to this unit from the creators of Cricket magazine, on the EduPlace web site.

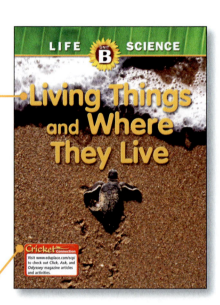

Reading in Science gives you something to think and talk about.

Chapters are parts of a unit. This tells you what the chapters are about.

You can read these on your own.

Discover! is a question to get you started. You can answer the question when you finish the unit.

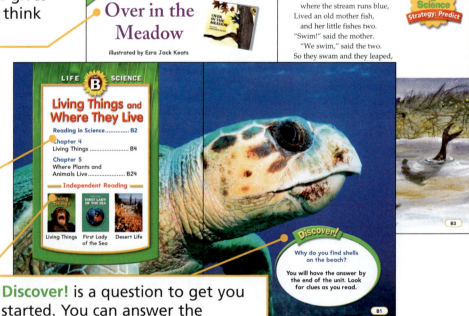

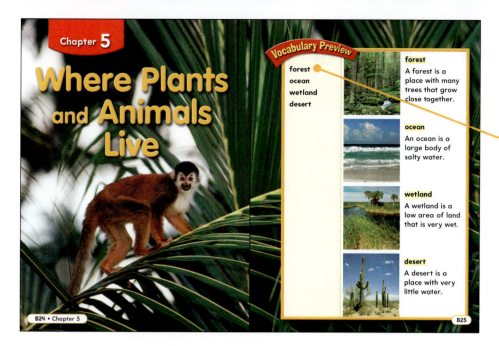

Chapter Vocabulary shows the vocabulary you will learn and gets you started.

Every lesson in your book has two parts.
Part 1: Investigate Activity

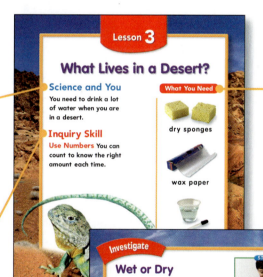

Science and You helps you think about the lesson.

Inquiry Skill shows the main inquiry skill for the activity and helps you use it.

What You Need to do the activity is shown here.

Steps to follow for the Investigate activity.

Think and Share lets you check what you have learned.

Investigate More lets you do more on your own.

xiii

Part 2: Learn by Reading

Vocabulary lists the new science words you will learn. In the text dark words with yellow around them are new words.

Main Idea is underlined to show you what is important.

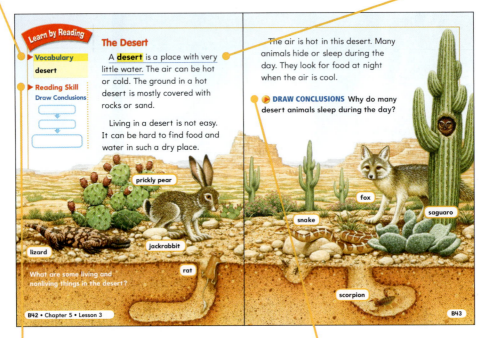

Reading Skill helps you understand the text.

Reading Skill Check has you think about what you just read.

Lesson Wrap-Up

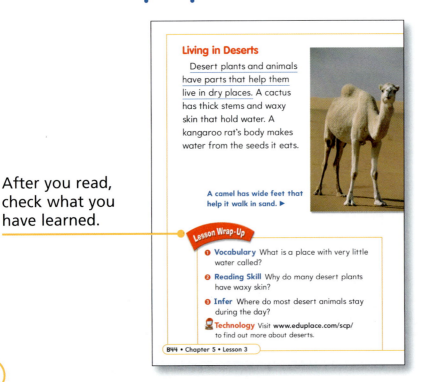

After you read, check what you have learned.

xiv

Focus On

Focus On lets you learn more about an important topic. Look for Biography, Technology, Literature, Readers' Theater—and more.

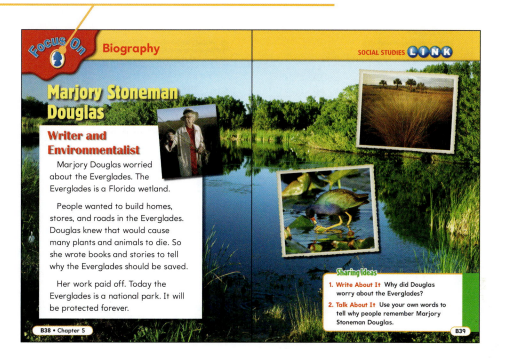

Links

Connects science to other subject areas.

You can do these at school or at home.

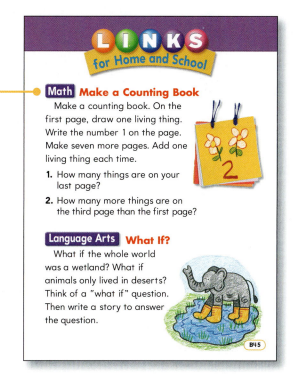

XV

Review and Test Prep

These reviews help you to know you are on track with your learning. Here you will practice and apply your new skills.

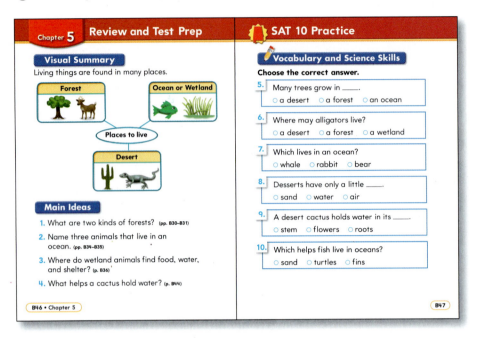

Unit Wrap-Up

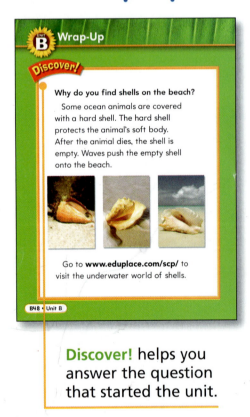

Discover! helps you answer the question that started the unit.

References

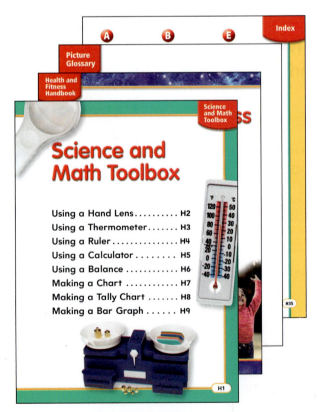

The back of your book includes sections you will refer to again and again.

The Nature of Science

Alabama

Science is an adventure.
People all over the world do
science. You can do science, too.
You probably already do.

Alabama Science Course of Study

Students will:

1. Select appropriate tools and technological resources needed to gather, analyze, and interpret data.
   Examples: platform balances, hand lenses, computers, maps, graphs, journals

2. Identify basic properties of objects.
   Examples: size, shape, color, texture

3. Describe effects of forces on objects, including change of speed, direction, and position.

4. Describe survival traits of living things, including color, shape, size, texture, and covering.
   - Classifying plants and animals according to physical traits
     Examples: animals—six legs on insects,
     plants—green leaves on evergreen trees
   - Identifying developmental stages of plants and animals
     Examples: plants—seed developing into seedling, seedling developing into tree;
     animals—piglet developing into pig, kid developing into goat
   - Describing a variety of habitats and natural homes of animals

5. Identify parts of the human body, including the head, neck, shoulders, arms, spine, and legs.
   - Recognizing the importance of a balanced diet for healthy bones
   - Discussing the relationship of muscles and bones to locomotion
   - Discussing the relationship of bones to protection of vital organs
     Example: protection of brain by skull
   - Identifying technology used by scientists to study the human body
     Examples: X-ray images, magnetic resonance imaging (MRI)

7. Identify components of Earth's surface, including soil, rocks, and water.

8. Recognize daily changes in weather, including clouds, precipitation, and temperature.
   - Recognizing instruments used to observe weather
     Examples: thermometer, rain gauge, wind sock, weather vane
   - Recording weather data using weather journals, charts, and maps

9. Identify ways to conserve Earth's resources.
   Example: turning off lights and water when not in use

10. Describe uses of recycled materials.
    Examples: manufacture of paper products from old newspapers, production of mulch from trees

11. Compare the day sky to the night sky as observed with the unaided eye.

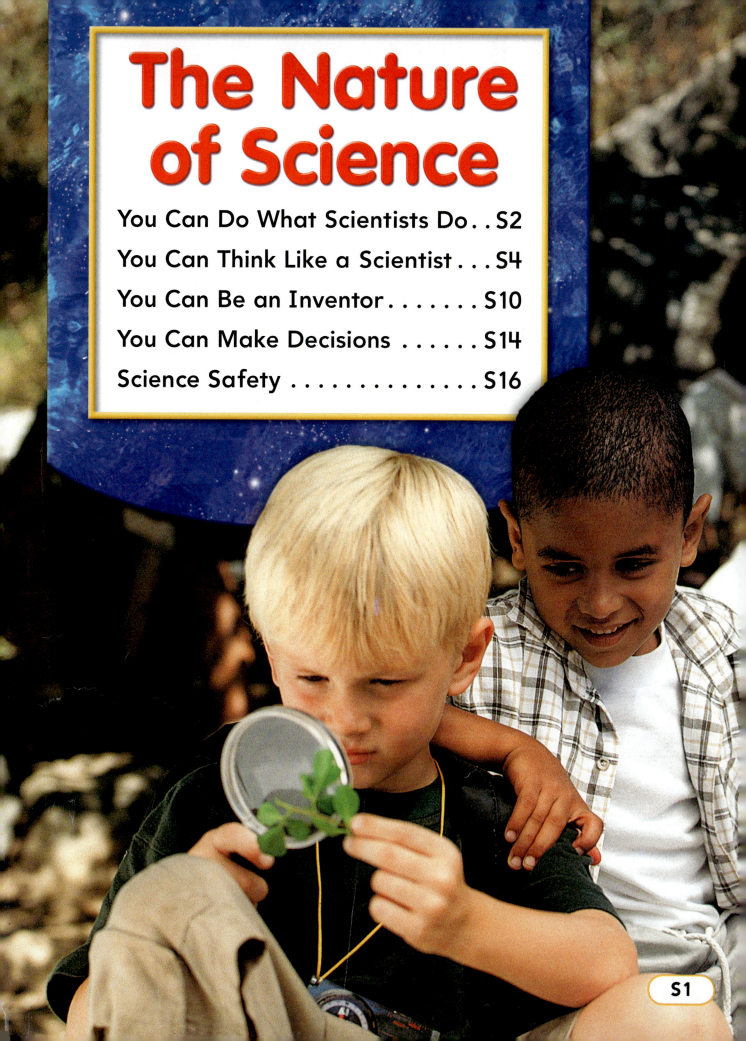

The Nature of Science

You Can Do What Scientists Do . . S2
You Can Think Like a Scientist . . . S4
You Can Be an Inventor S10
You Can Make Decisions S14
Science Safety S16

You Can...
Do What Scientists Do

Donna House planned this wetland and woods. Ms. House is a scientist. She studies plants and how native people use them. She protects plants that are in danger of dying out.

Scientists Investigate

Scientists ask questions. They answer them by observing and testing. Donna House gathers facts about plants. She reads about plants. She uses tools to measure plants. She talks to other scientists. She talks to elders in different tribes.

Donna House chose the wild plants around the National Museum of the American Indian in Washington, D.C.

Meet Donna House. She says you can learn a lot by taking walks outdoors with your elders.

You Can... Think Like a Scientist

Everyone can do science. To think like a scientist you have to:

- ask a lot of questions.
- work with others and listen to their ideas.
- try things over and over again.
- tell what really happens, not what you wanted to happen.

Do goldfish have eyelids? It looks like goldfish never close their eyes.

I read that goldfish do not have eyelids.

If the sunlight is too bright for their eyes, they swim to a shady spot.

Use Critical Thinking

Scientists use observations and other facts to answer their questions. A fact can be checked to make sure it is true. An opinion is what you think about the facts.

When you think, "That can't be true," you are thinking critically. Critical thinkers question what they hear.

You Can Think Like a Scientist

Science Inquiry

You can use **science inquiry** to learn about the world around you. Say you are playing with magnets.

Observe It seems like when I hold the magnets one way, they push apart. When I turn one magnet, they stick.

Ask a Question I wonder, are some parts of round magnets stronger than other parts?

Form an Idea I think some parts of round magnets are stronger than others.

Experiment I will need a round magnet and some paper clips. I will count how many paper clips the round magnet picks up. I will test different places on the magnet.

Conclusion I found that a round magnet picks up more paper clips on one side. So, my idea is supported. Round magnets do have parts that are stronger.

Communicate what you learn. You can use words or pictures. Tell others to try it themselves. You can expect them to get the same results.

You Can Think Like a Scientist

Inquiry Process

Here is how some scientists answer questions and make new discoveries.

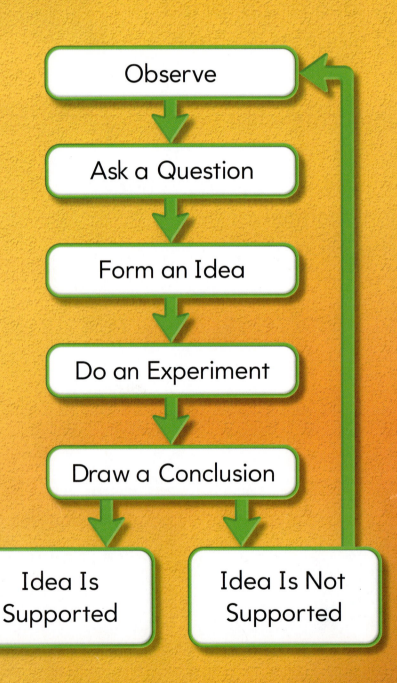

Try it Yourself!

Experiment With a Diving Squid

Squeeze the bottle. The squid sinks. Stop squeezing. The squid floats.

1. What questions do you have about the squid?

2. How would you find the answers?

3. Make a plan to test your idea. Tell what you think you will find out.

You Can...
Be an Inventor

Neil Dermody had trouble finding his seat belt when he was eight years old. His mom asked him to invent a way to solve the problem.

First, Neil thought of putting light bulbs on the seat belt. He decided that the bulbs might break. Then he thought of things that glow in the dark.

Neil painted the buckle with paint that glowed in the dark. He sewed glow-in-the-dark fabric to the strap. It worked just fine.

Neil Dermody wins first prize for his invention.

"My mom always said, 'What problem are you having? How can you fix it?'"

What Is Technology?

The tools people make and use are **technology**. Paint that glows in the dark is technology. So is a hybrid car.

Scientists use technology. They use telescopes to study things that are far from Earth. They also use tools to measure things.

Technology can make life easier. Sometimes it causes problems too. Cars make it easy for people to travel. But a car's gas and oil can pollute the air.

You Can Be An Inventor

A Better Idea

"I wish I had a better way to _____." How would you fill in the blank? Everyone can invent new things and ideas. Even you!

An electric toothbrush is fun to use. It also cleans teeth better.

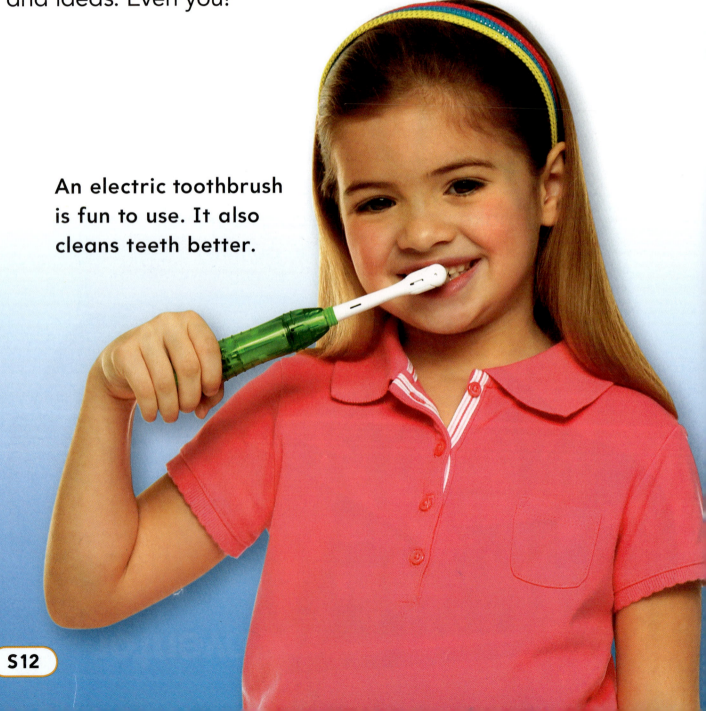

How to Be an Inventor

1. **Find a problem.** It may be at school, at home, or in your neighborhood.

2. **Think of a way to solve the problem.** List some ways to solve the problem. Decide which one will work best.

3. **Make a sample and try it out.** Your idea may need many materials or none at all. Try it out many times.

4. **Make your invention better.** Use what you learned to make changes.

5. **Share your invention.** Tell how your invention makes an activity easier or more fun. If it did not work well, tell why.

You Can... Make Decisions

Throwing Paper Away

How much paper does your class throw away? Most paper and other trash is buried in the ground. It takes up a lot of space.

Paper is made from mashed wood. Many trees are cut down to make paper. A lot of water is used. A lot of energy is used too.

Deciding What to Do

How could your class throw away less paper?

Here's how to make your decision. You can use the same steps to help solve problems in your home or neighborhood.

Learn → Learn about the problem. Find the facts. You could talk to an expert or read a book.

List → List actions you could take. Add actions other people could take.

Decide → Decide which action is best for you, your school, or your neighborhood.

Share → Tell others what you decide.

Science Safety

Know the safety rules of your classroom and follow them. Follow the safety tips in your science book.

- ▶ Wear safety goggles when your teacher tells you.
- ▶ Keep your work area clean. Tell your teacher about spills right away.
- ▶ Learn how to care for the plants and animals in your classroom.
- ▶ Wash your hands when you are done.

Contents

Plants and Animals — AL2–AL3
- American Alligator
- Yellowhammer
- Cotton Plant
- Blue Catfish

Environments — AL4–AL5
- Little River Canyon
- Cheaha Mountain
- Sequoyah Caverns
- Dauphin Island

Landmarks — AL6–AL7
- Southern Environmental Center
- Interactive Museum
- Woodlawn EcoScape

Map of Alabama — AL8

Alabama Fact File

Plants and Animals

American Alligator

Lives: freshwater swamps and marshes

Size: 10 to 14 feet

Teeth: 74 to 80

Eats: fish, turtles, small mammals, birds

Eggs: 20 to 50

Nests: on land near water

Yellowhammer

Type: woodpecker
Eats: insects, seeds, fruits
Nest: hole in a tree or stump
Eggs: 5 to 7
Wingspan: 18 to 21 inches

Cotton Plant

Appearance: leafy green shrub with pink and cream flowers
Seeds: surrounded by downy white fibers
Grown: in 59 counties
Uses: fiber, food, animal feed, fertilizer

Blue Catfish

Lives: rivers, swamps, reservoirs
Size: can be more than 100 pounds
Eats: crayfish, fish, mussels, snails, water insects
Age: about 14 years

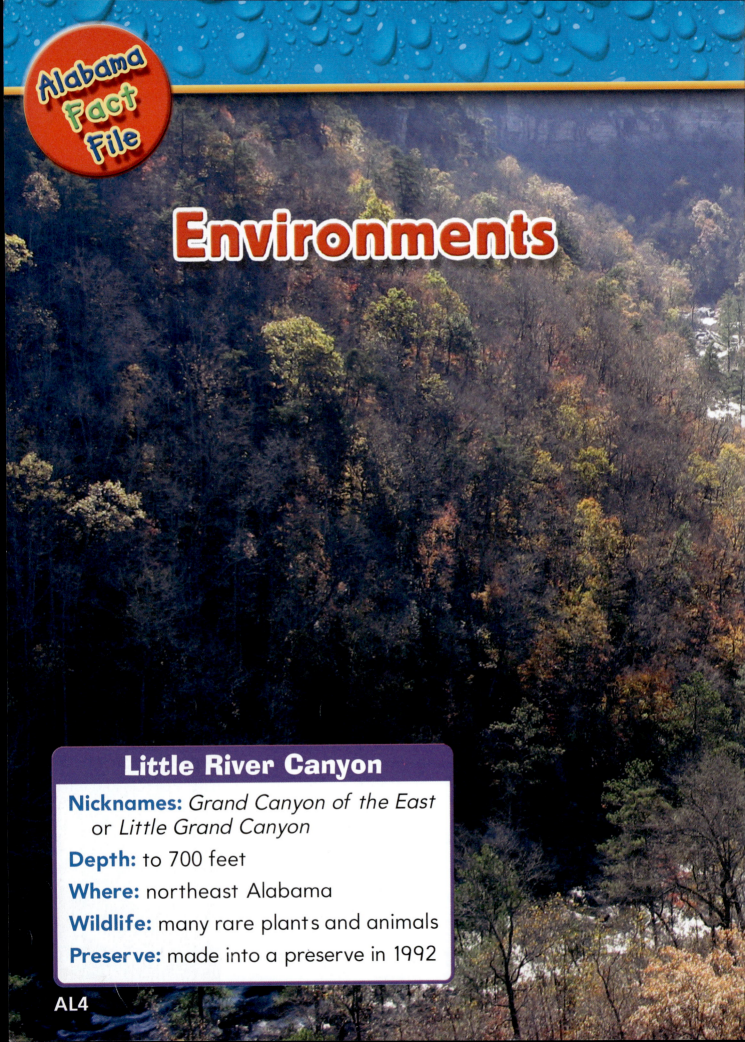

Alabama Fact File

Environments

Little River Canyon

Nicknames: *Grand Canyon of the East* or *Little Grand Canyon*

Depth: to 700 feet

Where: northeast Alabama

Wildlife: many rare plants and animals

Preserve: made into a preserve in 1992

Cheaha Mountain

Name: means *high place*

Height: 2,047 feet, highest point in Alabama

Where: Appalachian Plateau

Forest: surrounded by Talladega National Forest

Sequoyah Caverns

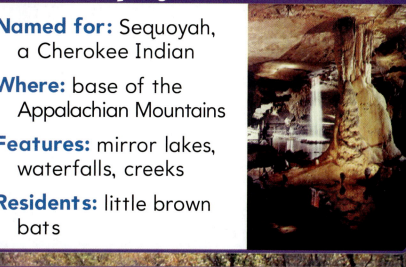

Named for: Sequoyah, a Cherokee Indian

Where: base of the Appalachian Mountains

Features: mirror lakes, waterfalls, creeks

Residents: little brown bats

Dauphin Island

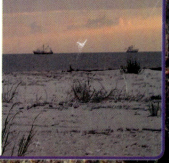

What: barrier island

Where: Gulf of Mexico

Sand: 95% quartz

Color: white

Coastline: 16 miles

Alabama Fact File

Landmarks

Southern Environmental Center

Where: Birmingham-Southern College, Birmingham

Hours: 9:00 a.m. to 5:00 p.m.

Exhibits: guided group tours of Interactive Museum, EcoScape Gardens

Special feature: largest educational facility of its kind in Alabama

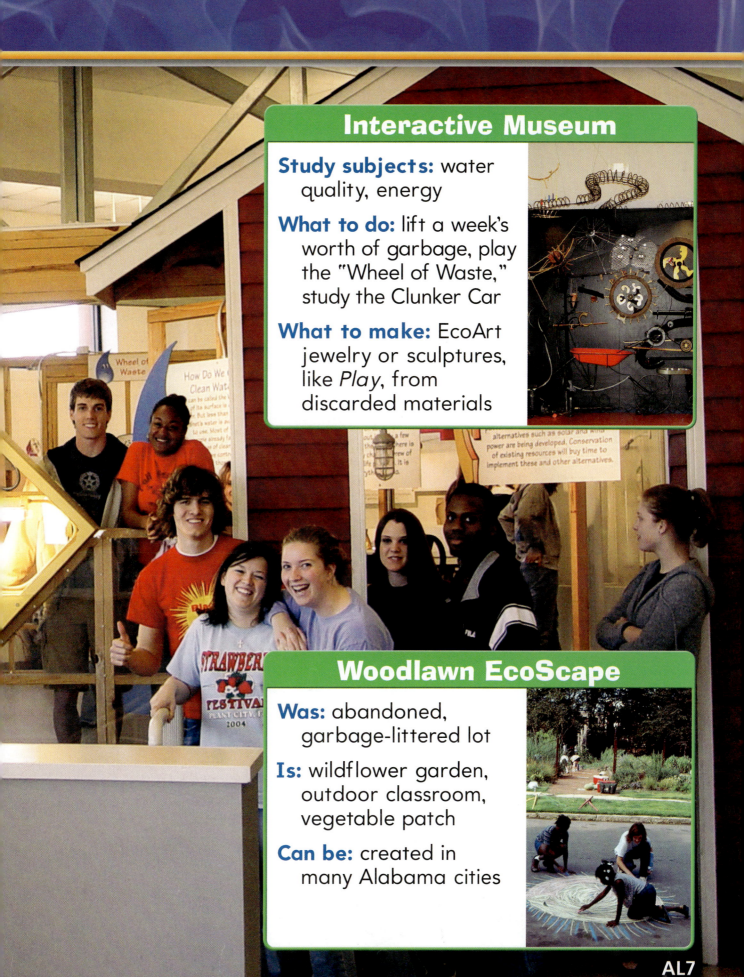

Interactive Museum

Study subjects: water quality, energy

What to do: lift a week's worth of garbage, play the "Wheel of Waste," study the Clunker Car

What to make: EcoArt jewelry or sculptures, like *Play*, from discarded materials

Woodlawn EcoScape

Was: abandoned, garbage-littered lot

Is: wildflower garden, outdoor classroom, vegetable patch

Can be: created in many Alabama cities

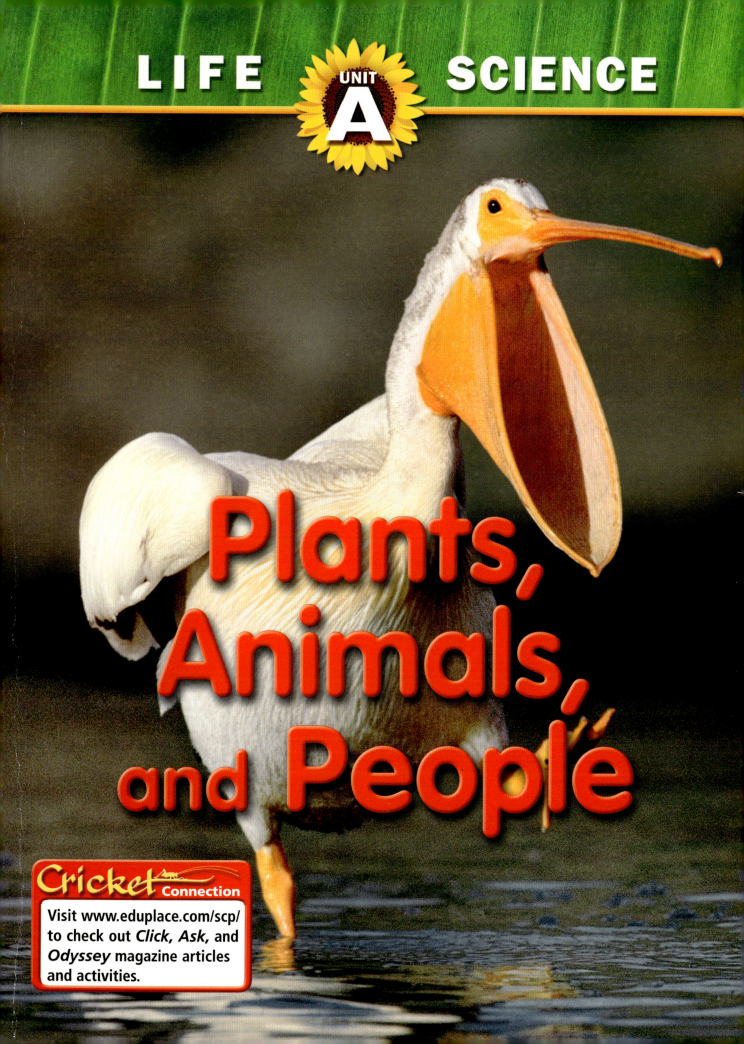

LIFE SCIENCE
UNIT A

Plants, Animals, and People

Reading in Science A2

Chapter 1
Plants A4

Chapter 2
Animals A28

Chapter 3
People A52

Independent Reading

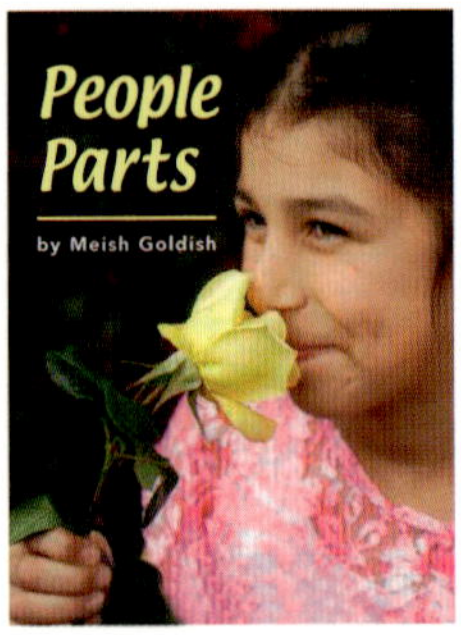

People Parts

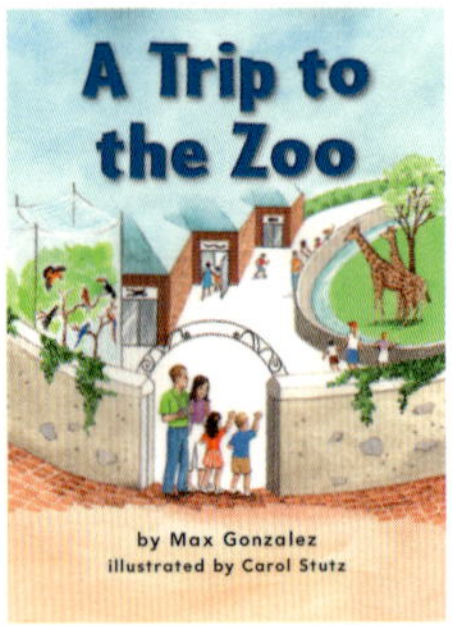

A Trip to the Zoo

Antonia Novello

Discover!

What bird flaps its wings the fastest?

Think about this question as you read. You will have the answer by the end of the unit.

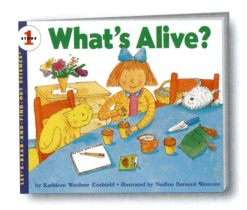

What's Alive?

by Kathleen Weidner Zoehfeld
illustrated by
Nadine Bernard Westcott

A flower can have petals of pink or yellow or red. You have no petals, and you won't grow as tall as a tree. But, like a flower and a tree, you are growing.

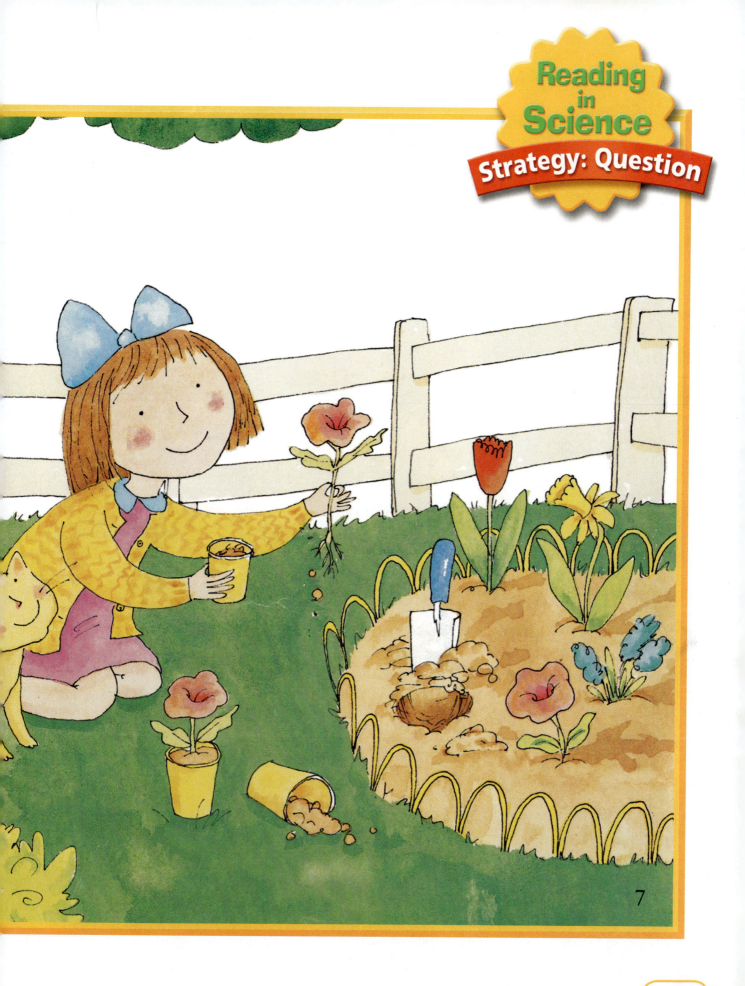

Chapter 1

Plants

Vocabulary Preview

- roots
- stem
- leaves
- flower
- seed
- spines
- life cycle
- cone
- seedling

roots
Roots are the parts of a plant that take in water from the ground.

seed
A seed has a new plant inside it.

spines
A cactus has sharp points called spines.

cone
Pine seeds grow in a cone.

Lesson 1

What Are the Parts of Plants?

Science and You
You can take better care of a plant when you know what it needs.

Inquiry Skill
Observe Use your senses to learn about things around you.

What You Need

paper towels and goggles

hand lens

plant

paper and crayons

Investigate

Observe a Plant

Steps

1. **Safety:** Wear goggles! Take the plant out of the pot. Carefully shake the dirt off the roots.

2. **Observe** Use a hand lens. Look at parts of the plant.

3. **Record Data** Draw a picture to show each plant part that you observe.

4. Put the plant back in the pot. **Safety:** Wash your hands!

STEP 1

STEP 2

STEP 3

Think and Share

1. What parts did you see when the plant was in the pot?
2. What part of the plant was in the soil?

Investigate More!

Ask Questions Finish the question. What would happen to the plant if it were missing its _____? Make a plan to find an answer.

Learn by Reading

Vocabulary

roots
stem
leaves
flower
seed

Reading Skill

Draw Conclusions

Plant Parts

Plants have parts. Most plants have roots, stems, and leaves. Some plants have flowers. Each part helps the plant in a different way.

Daisy

flower
leaf
stem
roots

Roots and Stems

Roots and stems help plants get what they need to grow. **Roots** take in water from the ground. They hold the plant in the ground.

A **stem** connects the roots to other plant parts. Stems carry water from the roots to the leaves and other plant parts. Stems also help hold a plant up.

▶ **DRAW CONCLUSIONS**
How does a stem help a plant?

roots

stem

Leaves

Most plants have leaves. The leaves make food for the plant. Leaves give off oxygen that people and animals breathe. Some leaves are food for people and animals.

How are the leaves different?

Flowers and Seeds

Many plants have flowers. A **flower** is a part of a plant that makes seeds. A **seed** has a new plant inside it. When a seed is planted, a new plant can grow.

These seeds grow in the flower.

▶ **DRAW CONCLUSIONS** Why are seeds important?

1. **Vocabulary** What are **roots**?

2. **Reading Skill** Why are a plant's roots under the ground?

3. **Observe** Which plant parts can you observe above the ground?

Technology Visit www.eduplace.com/scp/ to find out more about plant parts.

A11

Lesson 2

How Can Plants Be Sorted?

Science and You
Flowers, fruits, and leaves help you know what kind of plant you have.

Inquiry Skill
Compare Look for ways that objects are alike and different.

What You Need

leaves

paper

paper squares

glue and crayon

Investigate

Compare Leaves

Steps

1. **Compare** Look at leaves. See how they are alike and different.

2. **Record Data** Choose three leaves that are alike in one way. Make crayon rubbings of these leaves.

3. **Classify** Glue the rubbings on a sheet of paper. Write how the leaves are alike.

4. Repeat steps 2 and 3 with different leaves.

Think and Share

1. How are the leaves in each group alike?
2. How can you use plant parts to sort plants?

Investigate More!

Work Together Use your rubbings to make a class display. Add real leaves and pictures of leaves. Group the leaves that are alike.

A13

Learn by Reading

Vocabulary
spines

Reading Skill
Categorize and Classify

Sorting Plants

You can classify plants by looking at their parts. Some plants have flowers. Some plants have flat leaves. The stem of a tree is covered with bark. A cactus has sharp points called **spines**. You can also sort plants by looking at their roots and seeds.

▶ **CLASSIFY** What are three ways to sort plants?

How could you sort these plants?

A15

Eating Plants

Some plants are food for people. Farmers grow plants. Sometimes people grow plants for food in their own gardens. You can buy food plants in a grocery store, too. These plants are safe to eat. Not all plants are safe to eat.

Plants are food for animals, too. Some animals, such as deer and rabbits, eat leaves. Squirrels and some birds eat seeds.

▶ **DRAW CONCLUSIONS** How do plants help animals?

Some birds eat fruits.

Lesson Wrap-Up

1. **Vocabulary** What kind of plant has **spines**?
2. **Reading Skill** What are three plant parts that animals eat?
3. **Compare** How are plants different?
- **Technology** Visit www.eduplace.com/scp/ to find out more about sorting plants.

Focus On: Technology

Plant Power!

People use all parts of plants—seeds, roots, stems, leaves, and flowers.

Stems Wood from the stems of trees is used to make houses—even tree houses!

SOCIAL STUDIES **LINK**

Plant Parts	Things made from plant parts
Seeds The corn for your cornflakes comes from corn seeds.	cereal
Roots The roots of some beets are used to make sugar.	sugar
Leaves You use mint leaves if your toothpaste tastes like mint.	toothpaste
Flowers Many flowers are used to add pleasant smells to perfumes.	perfume

Sharing Ideas

1. **Write About It** Write a story about things in your home that are made from plant stems.
2. **Talk About It** Talk about things in your classroom that are made from plants.

Lesson 3

How Do Plants Change as They Grow?

Science and You
You have grown from a baby to a child. Plants grow and change, too.

Inquiry Skill
Use Models Use pictures to learn about real objects.

What You Need

plant pictures

Investigate

Use Plant Models

Steps

1. **Observe** Look closely at plant pictures. Think about how the plant grows.

2. **Use Models** Order the pictures to show how the plant starts, grows, and dies.

3. Make a list to show five steps in this plant's life.

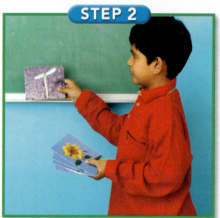

Think and Share

1. What is the first step of this plant's life?

2. Describe how the plant changes through its life.

Investigate More!

Experiment Do all plants grow at the same speed? Plant two kinds of seeds at the same time. See which one grows the fastest.

Learn by Reading

Vocabulary
life cycle
cone
seedling

Reading Skill
Sequence

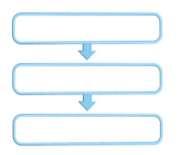

Plant Life Cycles

Every living thing has a life cycle. A **life cycle** is the order of changes that happen in the lifetime of a plant or animal. The life cycle of a tree takes years. The life cycle of a dandelion only takes months. When the plants grow up, they will look like their parents.

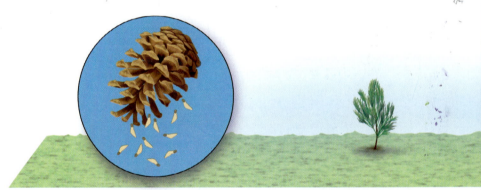

Pine Tree

Pine seeds grow in a **cone**.

A seed grows into a **seedling**, or a young plant.

Dandelion

seeds   seedling

🔸 **SEQUENCE** How do plants change as they grow?

The seedling grows into a tree.

The tree and cones grow.

The life cycle begins again with new seeds.

growing plant

flowers grow

new seeds

◀ **6 months old**

Plant Lives

Plants live for different lengths of time. Some live only for a few months. Some plants live for about two years. Other plants live for many years.

3,000 years old ▶

Lesson Wrap-Up

① **Vocabulary** What is a **cone**?

② **Reading Skill** What comes after the seed in a plant's life cycle?

③ **Use Models** How can a model help you learn about a plant's life cycle?

Technology Visit www.eduplace.com/scp/ to find out more about plant life cycles.

LINKS for Home and School

Math — Find a Pattern

Look at the pattern of the leaves.

1. What is the pattern?
2. What color is likely to come next?

Music — Sing a Plant Song

Sing these words to the tune of "The Farmer in the Dell." Then make up more verses about a plant life cycle.

The farmer plants a seed,
The farmer plants a seed,
Hi-ho, the garden-o,
The farmer plants a seed.

Chapter 1 Review and Test Prep

Visual Summary

Plants are living things. They can be grouped by plant parts.

Plant Parts

Plants have different parts.

roots | stem | leaves | flowers

Main Ideas

1. How do roots and stems help a plant? (p. A9)

2. How do plant leaves help people and animals? (p. A10)

3. What is one way to group plants? (p. A14)

4. How does a plant change during its life cycle? (p. A22–A23)

SAT 10 Practice

Vocabulary and Science Skills

Choose the correct answer.

5. Which plant part makes seeds?
   ○ roots   ○ flowers   ○ stems

6. All plants have ____.
   ○ flowers   ○ cones   ○ life cycles

7. Where do people grow plants to eat?
   ○ zoo   ○ garden   ○ store

8. A new plant grows from a ____.
   ○ seed   ○ spine   ○ leaf

9. Which is a part of a plant's life cycle?
   ○ spine   ○ seedling   ○ stem

10. Plants give off oxygen through their ____.
    ○ leaves   ○ stems   ○ roots

A27

Chapter 2

Animals

A28 • Chapter 2

Vocabulary Preview

wings
fins
mammal
lungs
gills
reptile
amphibian
adult

fins
Fins are body parts that help a fish move.

mammal
A mammal is an animal whose mother makes milk to feed her babies.

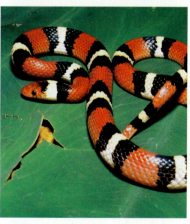

reptile
A reptile is an animal that has dry skin with scales.

adult
An adult is a full-grown plant, animal, or person.

Lesson 1

How Do Animals Use Their Parts?

Science and You
A lizard uses its tail and legs like you use your hands.

Inquiry Skill
Infer Use what you know and what you observe to tell what you think.

What You Need

backgrounds

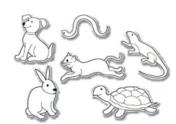

animal cutouts

crayons

glue

Investigate

Hidden Animals

Steps

1. **Observe** Look at a background. Color an animal so that it looks like the background.

2. Glue your animal on the background to hide it.

3. **Compare** Trade pictures with a classmate. Try to find the hidden animal.

Think and Share

1. Why was the paper animal able to hide on the background?

2. **Infer** Tell how you think an animal's body color helps it hide outside.

Investigate More!

Ask Questions How might an animal's body shape help it hide? Finish this question. How does a _____'s body shape help it hide?

Learn by Reading

Animal Body Parts

Vocabulary
wings
fins

Reading Skill
Main Idea and Details

Animals have body parts that help them find food and stay safe. Animals use their eyes, ears, noses, legs, tails, and other parts to help them live.

Bush Baby

Large eyes help it see at night.

Ears help it find insects to eat.

Gray fur helps it hide in trees.

Legs and fingers help it catch food and hold onto trees.

Some animals can use body parts to hurt other animals or scare them away. Some animals have colors or shapes that help them hide.

Using Body Parts to Stay Safe

quills

stinger

claws and teeth

smell

sound

color and shape

▶ **MAIN IDEA** What body parts help animals find food?

Parts for Moving

Animals have body parts that help them move. A bird has **wings** that help it fly through the air. A bird also has legs that help it walk, hop, and hold on to trees.

A fish has a tail and **fins** that help it move. A lion has strong legs that help it run and climb.

▶ **MAIN IDEA** How does a bird use its legs?

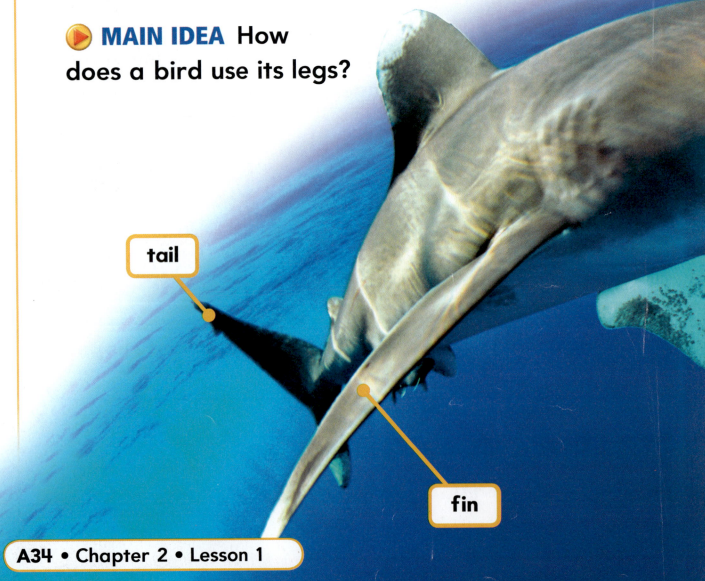

tail

fin

leg

wing

Lesson Wrap-Up

1. **Vocabulary** How do **fins** help a fish?

2. **Reading Skill** What are some ways in which body parts help animals?

3. **Infer** How does body color help an animal stay safe?

Technology Visit www.eduplace.com/scp/ to find out more about animal body parts.

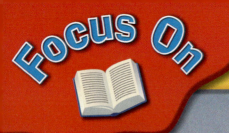

Focus On Literature

Read to find out about the snowshoe hare in winter and in summer.

In a Winter Meadow

by Jack Prelutsky

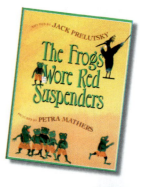

In a winter meadow
icy breezes blow,
snowshoe hares are running
softly through the snow.

Up and down they scurry,
darting left and right,
snowshoe hares are running,
dressed in winter white.

READING LINK

Animal Disguises

by Belinda Weber

Snowshoe hares live in Alaska. In the summer their coats are brown in order to blend in with the ground. In the winter the hares grow new, white coats to help them stay hidden in the snow.

Sharing Ideas

1. **Write About It** How are snowshoe hares protected in winter?

2. **Talk About It** Why does the snowshoe hare's color change in summer?

Lesson 2

How Are Animals Grouped?

Science and You
The birds, turtles, and squirrels you see in a park are in different animal groups.

Inquiry Skill
Classify Group objects that are alike in some way.

What You Need

animal pictures

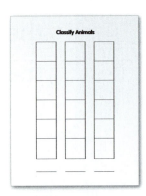

graph paper

crayons

Investigate

Classify Animals

Steps

1. **Classify** Sort animal pictures into groups that are alike in some way.

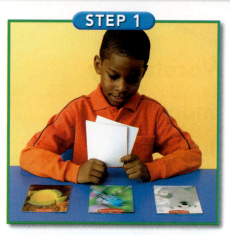
STEP 1

2. **Record Data** Make a graph to show your groups. Label each group. Color in one block on your graph for every animal.

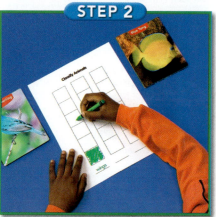
STEP 2

3. **Communicate** Tell how you sorted the animals. Tell how many animals are in each group.

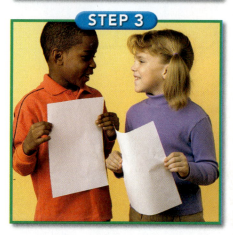
STEP 3

Think and Share

1. How are the animals in a group alike?
2. How can you use body parts to group animals?

Investigate More!

Solve a Problem Suppose you have a friend who has never seen a turtle. How would you tell your friend what a turtle looks like?

A39

Learn by Reading

Vocabulary

mammal
lungs
gills
reptile
amphibian

Reading Skill
Compare and Contrast

Mammals

Some scientists study how animals are alike and different. They group animals that have like body parts.

One group of animals is called mammals. A **mammal** is an animal whose mother makes milk to feed her babies. Most mammals have hair or fur. They have **lungs**, or body parts that take in air.

Birds and Fish

Birds and fish do not have all the same body parts that mammals have. Birds have wings to fly. A bird's body is covered with feathers. Birds have mouth parts called bills.

A fish lives in water. **Gills** are the parts of a fish that help it breathe underwater.

▲ A bird uses lungs to breathe.

▶ **COMPARE AND CONTRAST**
What body parts do mammals, birds, and fish use to breathe?

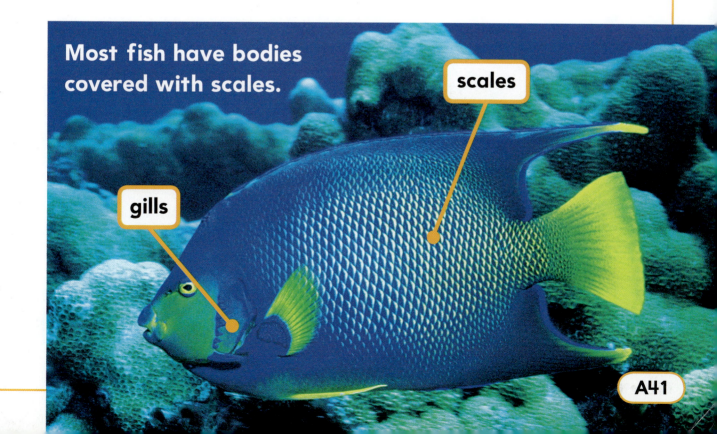

Most fish have bodies covered with scales.

scales

gills

Reptiles and Amphibians

Reptiles and amphibians look different from mammals and birds. A **reptile** is an animal that has dry skin with scales. It has lungs for breathing. Snakes, lizards, and turtles are reptiles.

An **amphibian** is an animal that has wet skin with no hair, feathers, or scales. It spends some time in water and some time on land. Frogs, toads, and salamanders are amphibians.

What Animals Eat

You can group animals by what they eat. Some animals eat plants. Some eat other animals. Some animals eat plants and animals.

Animals that eat other animals have sharp teeth.

Animals that only eat plants have flat teeth.

▶ **COMPARE AND CONTRAST** How are the teeth of animals different?

Lesson Wrap-Up

1. **Vocabulary** What are gills?
2. **Reading Skill** How are fish and reptiles alike?
3. **Classify** Which animal is an amphibian—a snake, a frog, or a fish?

Technology Visit www.eduplace.com/scp/ to find out more about animal groups.

Lesson 3

How Do Animals Grow and Change?

Science and You
A tiny kitten grows up to be an adult cat.

Inquiry Skill
Use Models Use pictures to learn about real objects.

What You Need

cat pictures

Investigate

A Cat's Life Cycle

Steps

1. **Observe** Look at pictures of a growing cat. See how the pictures are different.

2. **Use Models** Order the cat pictures from youngest to oldest.

3. **Communicate** Use the pictures to tell a friend about a cat's life cycle.

Think and Share

1. Which picture shows the youngest cat?

2. **Compare** How does the cat look different in the first and last pictures?

Investigate More!

Ask Questions What else do you want to know about how an animal grows? Find someone to help you get an answer. Share what you learn.

A45

Learn by Reading

Vocabulary
adult

Reading Skill
Sequence

Animal Life Cycles

Animals go through changes called a life cycle. First, an animal is born or hatches from an egg. Then it grows to be an adult. An **adult** is a full-grown plant, animal, or person. A life cycle begins again when an adult animal has babies.

Life Cycle of a Salamander

eggs

ready to hatch

Some animals grow faster than others. Salamanders become adults in about 3 months. Elephants take 20 years to grow up.

▶ **SEQUENCE** What part of a salamander's life cycle comes after the adult?

growing

adult

Parents and Young Animals

Adult animals can become parents of baby animals. Some young animals look like their parents when they are born. A puppy looks like its parents. A frog does not look like its parents until it is an adult.

These puppies do not look exactly like their mother. ▶

Lesson Wrap-Up

① **Vocabulary** What is an **adult**?

② **Reading Skill** How does an animal's life cycle begin?

③ **Use Models** How can pictures help you understand an animal's life cycle?

🖥️ **Technology** Visit www.eduplace.com/scp/ to find out more about animal life cycles.

LINKS for Home and School

Math — Story Problems

Jane took a walk. She saw birds, bees, cats, and worms.

1. How many animals with wings did Jane see?
2. Use the chart. Write an animal story problem. Then solve a partner's story problem.

Language Arts — Animal Names

The words below are names for groups of animals. Draw a picture of a group. Then write a sentence about your picture.

gaggle of geese   pride of lions
kindle of kittens   swarm of bees
pod of whales   herd of elephants
school of fish

A female cat has a kindle of kittens.

Chapter 2 Review and Test Prep

Visual Summary

There are different kinds of animals. They grow in different ways.

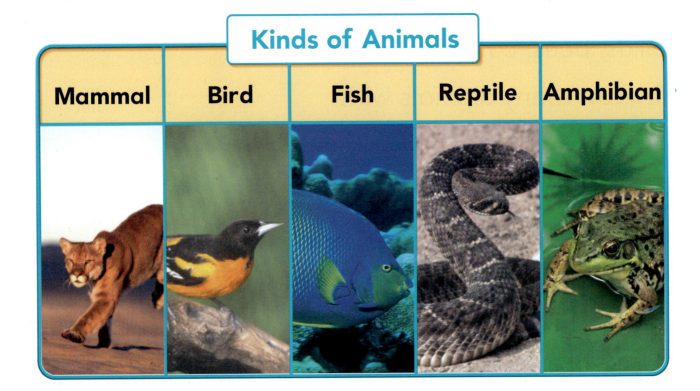

Kinds of Animals
Mammal | Bird | Fish | Reptile | Amphibian

Main Ideas

1. How does a fish move? (p. A34)

2. How can you use teeth to group animals? (p. A43)

3. What is a full-grown animal called? (p. A46)

4. How are animal life cycles different? (p. A47)

SAT 10 Practice

Vocabulary and Science Skills

Choose the correct answer.

5. Which helps a bush baby hide in trees?
   ○ ears   ● fur   ○ eyes

6. Which help fish breathe?
   ○ gills   ● scales   ○ fins

7. Which has dry skin and scales?
   ○ mammal   ● bird   ○ reptile

8. Which lives in water and on land?
   ○ frog   ○ lion   ● owl

9. Which body parts help a bird move?
   ○ ears   ○ teeth   ● wings

10. Animals that only eat plants have ____.
    ○ sharp teeth   ● flat teeth   ○ long teeth

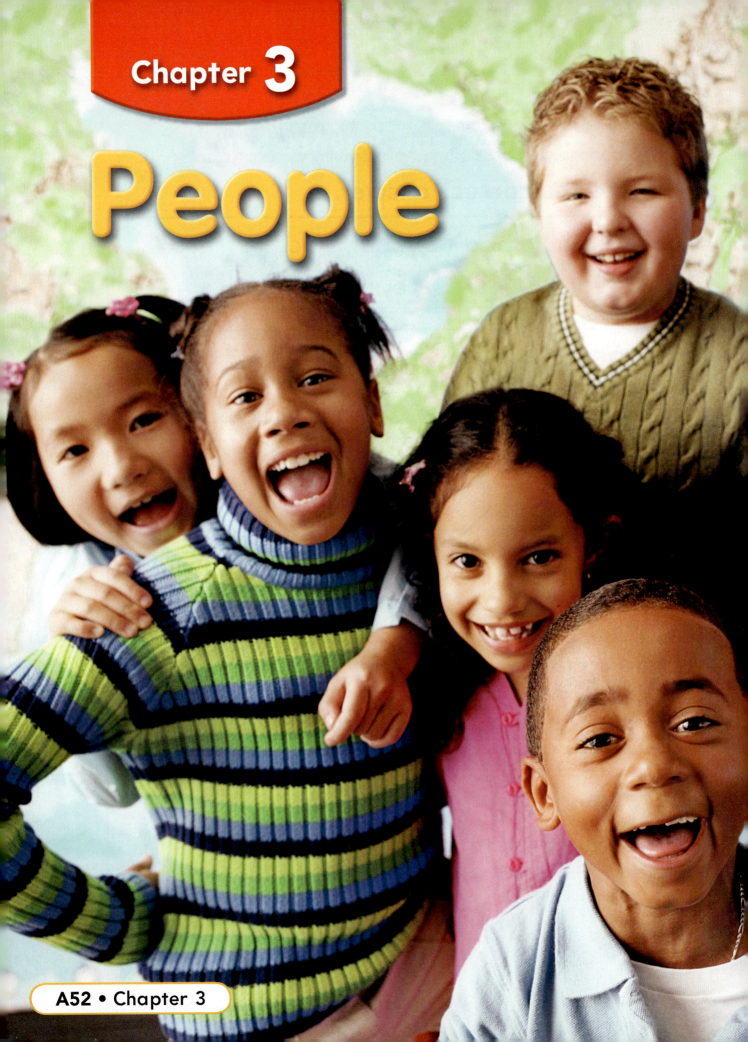

Vocabulary Preview

senses
infant
teen
exercise
sleep

senses
Your senses help you see, hear, smell, taste, and feel things.

infant
A new baby is called an infant.

teen
A teen is a person between 13 and 19 years old.

exercise
Exercise is movement that keeps your body strong.

Lesson 1

How Do People Use Their Parts?

Science and You
Your body has parts that help you move and do other things.

Inquiry Skill
Communicate Share with others what you learn and observe.

What You Need

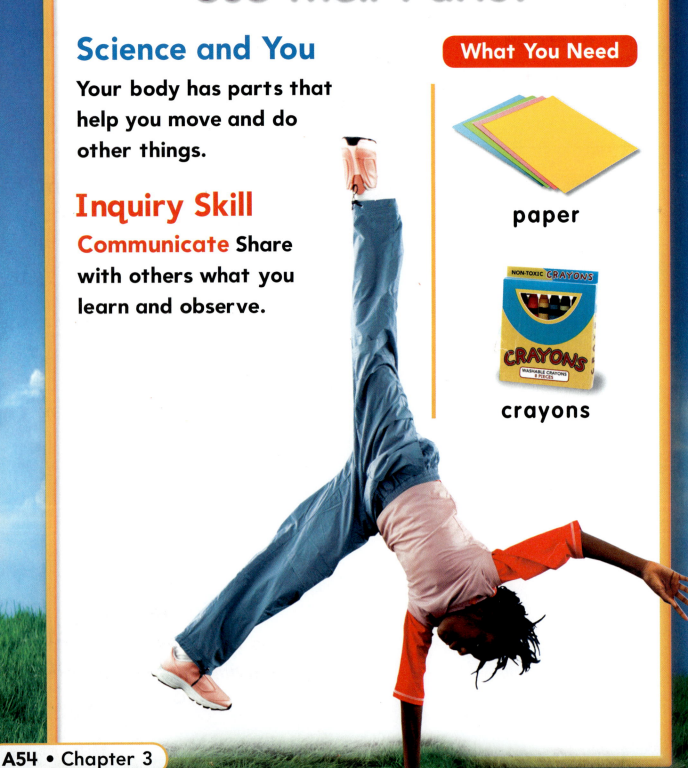

paper

crayons

Investigate

Model Your Body

Steps

1. Draw a picture of yourself.

2. **Use Models** Draw a line to each body part on your picture. Label each part.

3. **Communicate** Share your picture with a partner. Name each body part, and tell what it does.

STEP 1

STEP 2

STEP 3

Think and Share

1. How did your hands help you with the picture?

2. Pick one body part that you drew. Tell what it does.

Investigate More!

Experiment You hear with your ears. Close your eyes for one minute. Listen. Then list what you heard.

Learn by Reading

Vocabulary
senses

Reading Skill
Draw Conclusions

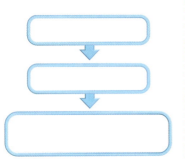

Your Senses

You have **senses** that help you feel, smell, hear, see, and taste things. Different body parts are used for each sense. Your senses help keep you safe. They also help you learn about the world.

▶ **DRAW CONCLUSIONS** How do you think popcorn feels, looks, and sounds?

You use your hands to feel.

A56 • Chapter 3 • Lesson 1

Other Body Parts

Your body parts work together to help you do things. You use your arms and legs to ride a bike. Hands and arms help you draw.

Many animals have body parts like yours. A cat has eyes, ears, a nose, a mouth, and legs. So do you. A cat also has paws. You do not. You have hands and feet.

mouth to talk and eat

▲ arms and hands to hold

legs to walk and run ▶

🔴 **DRAW CONCLUSIONS** What body parts help you play on a playground?

Lesson Wrap-Up

❶ Vocabulary How do your **senses** help you?

❷ Reading Skill How do people and lions use their legs?

❸ Communicate How can you share what you know about people's body parts?

🖥️ **Technology** Visit www.eduplace.com/scp/ to find out more about your body parts.

Focus On: Health and Safety

Be Active

Your body has parts that help you move. To have a healthy body, you need to put those parts to work!

▶ biking

▲ bending and stretching

Bending and stretching help your body move easily. Running, biking, swimming, and jumping rope keep your heart and muscles strong. Find a way to be active every day.

jumping rope ▶

Sharing Ideas

1. **Write About It** Write about different ways that you moved your body today.

2. **Talk About It** Talk with a partner. List three ways that you can be active every day.

Lesson 2

How Do People Grow and Change?

Science and You
You will keep growing until you are an adult.

Inquiry Skill
Work Together Share what you observe with a partner.

What You Need

pictures

Investigate

A Person's Life

Steps

1. **Observe** Look at pictures of a person.

2. **Compare** Order the pictures to show how the person changed as she grew.

3. **Communicate** Tell a partner how the pictures show the changes in the life cycle of a person.

STEP 1

STEP 2

STEP 3

Think and Share

1. What is the beginning of a person's life?

2. **Infer** What is one way that a person changes as he or she grows?

Investigate More!

Work Together Spread out your hand. Have a friend measure from your little finger to your thumb. Then measure an adult's hand. Share what you learn.

Learn by Reading

Vocabulary

infant
teen
exercise
sleep

Reading Skill

Sequence

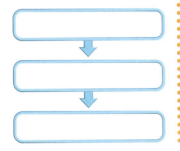

People Grow and Change

People grow and change all through their lives. You were an **infant**, or baby, when you were born. Then you grew and learned to walk and talk. You kept growing and started going to school. All this time, your family took care of you. They helped you learn new things.

infant

toddler

school-age child

You will grow to be a teen. A **teen** is a person between 13 and 19 years old. Next, you will become an adult.

You will take care of yourself when you are an adult. Your body will stop growing taller.

▶ **SEQUENCE** When will you become a teen?

Eat and Exercise for Health

You need to eat and exercise to stay healthy. Food gives you energy to live and grow. Things like fruits, vegetables, and milk help your body grow strong.

Foods to Eat

Eat More of These Foods	Eat Less of These Foods

Exercise is movement that keeps your body strong. Running and jumping make your bones and muscles strong. They also make your lungs and heart strong.

▶ **DRAW CONCLUSIONS** Why do you need to exercise?

How are these children exercising?

Get Enough Sleep

People need sleep. You rest your body and mind when you **sleep**. A good night's sleep will help you stay healthy and have lots of energy. Children in first grade need about ten hours of sleep each night.

Lesson Wrap-Up

1. **Vocabulary** What is one kind of **exercise**?
2. **Reading Skill** What do people grow to be after they are teens?
3. **Work Together** Talk to a friend about how an infant is different from an adult.

Technology Visit www.eduplace.com/scp/ to find out more about people growing and changing.

Math — Make a Pictograph

Look at the chart of children's favorite fruits.

| Mr. William's Class ||
Favorite Fruit	Tally
apple	III
grapes	IIII
banana	II
watermelon	I

Make a picture graph to show the data from the chart in a different way.

Social Studies — World Foods

Americans eat many foods that are popular in other countries. People in Mexico like tamales. Pasta is a favorite in Italy. Fried bananas are treats in Africa. Write about your family's favorite foods.

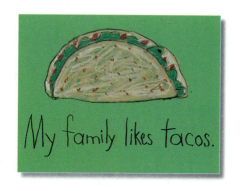

My family likes tacos.

Chapter 3 Review and Test Prep

Visual Summary

People are living things that have needs.

Healthful Habits

Food · Exercise · Sleep

Main Ideas

1. What do your senses do? (p. A56)

2. For which of the senses do you use your nose? (p. A57)

3. What does food do for you? (p. A66)

4. How much sleep does a first-grader need? (p. A68)

SAT 10 Practice

Vocabulary and Science Skills

Choose the correct answer.

5. Which gives your body rest?
   ○ senses   ○ exercise   ○ sleep

6. Which do you use to smell?
   ○ eyes   ○ nose   ○ mouth

7. When you are born, you are ____.
   ○ an adult   ○ a teen   ○ an infant

8. Exercise keeps your body ____.
   ○ tall   ○ strong   ○ rested

9. Food gives you ____.
   ○ energy   ○ exercise   ○ sleep

10. Which body part is most like a cat's paws?
    ○ legs   ○ feet   ○ arms

Wrap-Up

What bird flaps its wings the fastest?

A hummingbird flaps its wings about 75 times every second! The wings move so fast that they make a humming sound. Hummingbirds are called nature's helicopters because of the way they move.

Go to **www.eduplace.com/scp/** to learn more about the parts of a hummingbird.

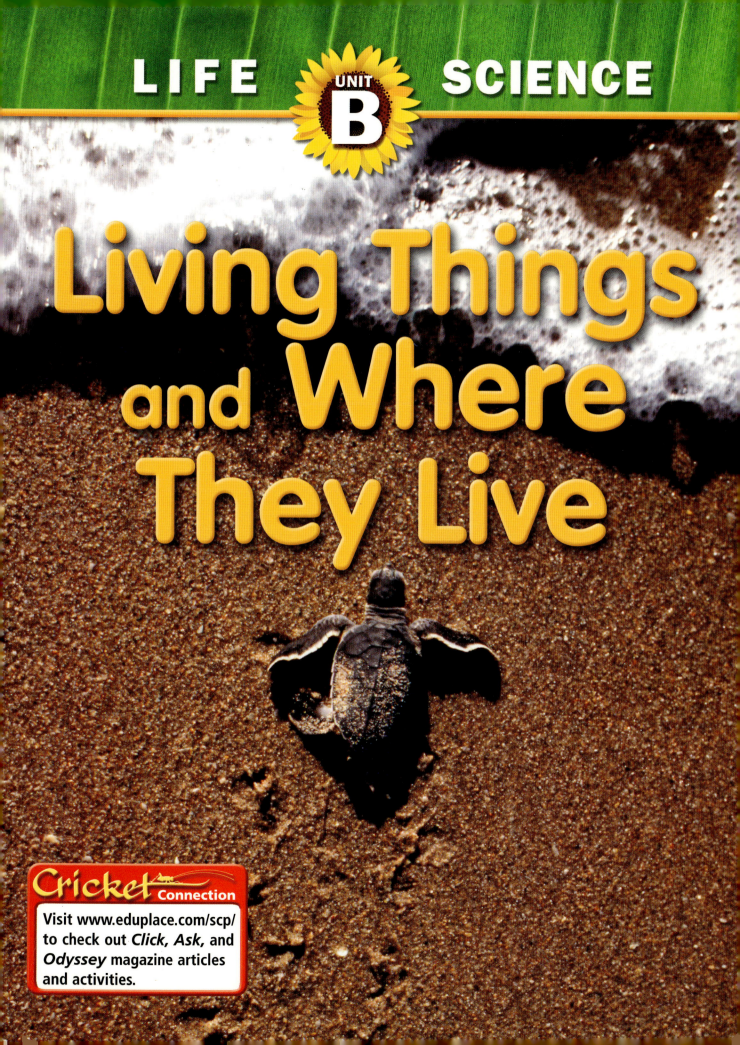

LIFE SCIENCE
UNIT B

Living Things and Where They Live

Reading in Science B2

Chapter 4
Living Things B4

Chapter 5
Where Plants and
Animals Live B24

Independent Reading

Living Things

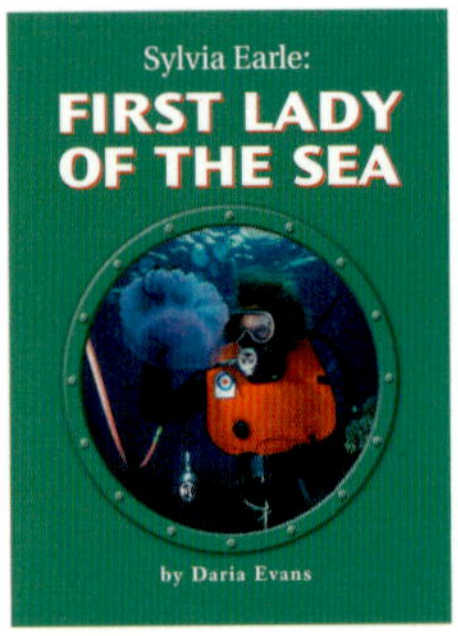

First Lady of the Sea

Desert Life

Discover!

Why do you find shells on the beach?

Think about this question as you read. You will have the answer by the end of the unit.

Over in the Meadow

illustrated by Ezra Jack Keats

B2 • Unit B

Over in the meadow
   where the stream runs blue,
Lived an old mother fish,
   and her little fishes two.
"Swim!" said the mother.
   "We swim," said the two.
So they swam and they leaped,
   Where the stream runs blue.

Vocabulary Preview

living thing
nonliving thing
food
sunlight
shelter

living thing
A living thing grows, changes, and makes other living things like itself.

nonliving thing
A nonliving thing does not eat, drink, grow, and make other things like itself.

food
Food is what living things use to get energy.

shelter
Shelter is a safe place for animals to live.

Lesson 1

What Is a Living Thing?

Science and You
You and your pets are living things.

Inquiry Skill
Classify Group objects that are alike in some way.

What You Need

objects

crayons and paper

Investigate

Classify Objects

Steps

1. **Observe** Look for ways in which some objects are alike or different.

2. **Classify** Sort the objects into groups that are alike in one way.

3. **Record Data** Draw a picture of the objects in each group. Write the names of your groups.

STEP 1

STEP 2

STEP 3

Think and Share

1. How are the objects in each group alike?

2. **Compare** How do your groups compare to those of the rest of the class?

Investigate More!

Work Together Cut out pictures of objects from magazines. Talk with a partner about a rule for sorting the objects. Then use the rule.

B7

Learn by Reading

Vocabulary

living thing
nonliving thing

Reading Skill

Main Idea and Details

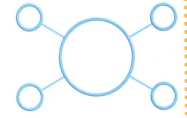

Living Things

A **living thing** grows, changes, and makes other living things like itself. It needs air, food, water, and space to stay alive.

People, birds, and squirrels are living things. Flowers, trees, and grass are living things, too. They all grow and change. They can make more living things like themselves.

▶ **MAIN IDEA** What does a living thing do?

The squirrel is a living thing.

The children, the trees, and the grass are living things.

Nonliving Things

A **nonliving thing** does not eat, drink, grow, and make other things like itself. It does not need food, water, and air. Rocks, bikes, and clothes are all nonliving things.

◀ living things

◀ nonliving thing

The girl is a living thing.
The doll is a nonliving thing.

Some nonliving things may act like living things. A fire grows. A fire needs air to burn. It takes up space. But fire does not need food or water. A fire is a nonliving thing.

▶ **MAIN IDEA** What is a nonliving thing?

fire

Lesson Wrap-Up

1. **Vocabulary** What is a **living thing**?
2. **Reading Skill** Name three nonliving things.
3. **Classify** Is water a living thing or a nonliving thing? Explain your answer.

 **Technology** Visit www.eduplace.com/scp/ to find out more about living and nonliving things.

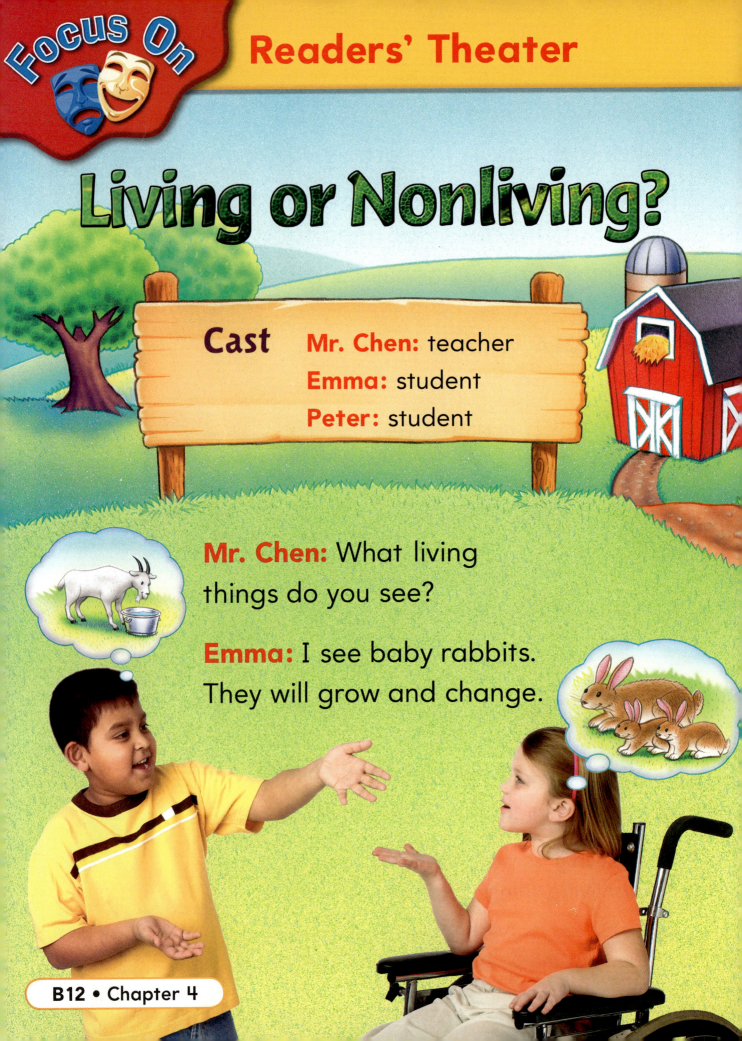

READING LINK

Peter: I see a goat drinking water from a pail. The goat is living. The pail and the water are not.

Mr. Chen: Right! How do you know?

Peter: Well, the goat needs water and air. That means it is living.

Emma: The goat also needs food and space to grow. The pail does not need those things.

Mr. Chen: Maybe all living things need nonliving things.

Emma: I am a living thing that needs a nonliving thing. I need lunch!

Sharing Ideas

1. **Write About It** Write a story about the living and nonliving things in a park.
2. **Talk About It** What are some nonliving things that it would be difficult to live without?

Lesson 2

What Do Living Things Need?

Science and You
Knowing the needs of living things helps you take care of them.

Inquiry Skill
Observe Use your senses to find out about objects.

What You Need

goggles

terrarium supplies

plants

water

Investigate

Observe Plants

Steps

1. **Safety:** Wear goggles! Use gravel, soil, and plants to make a terrarium like the one in the picture.

2. Spray a little water on the soil.

3. Cover the terrarium. Put the terrarium in a sunny place. **Safety:** Wash your hands after you finish!

4. **Observe** Look at the plants every day for one week. Record what you see.

Think and Share

1. **Infer** Are the plants living things? How do you know?
2. What do plants need?

Investigate More!

Ask Questions How much light do your plants need? Finish this question: What would happen to the plants if I _____? Make a plan for finding an answer.

Learn by Reading

Vocabulary
food
sunlight
shelter

Reading Skill
Categorize and Classify

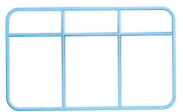

Food

Food is what living things use to get energy. Plants and animals need food.

Plants use sunlight, air, and water to make their own food. **Sunlight** is energy from the Sun. Most plants die if they do not get sunlight.

These cows are eating plants.

Animals eat food when they are hungry. Some animals eat plants. Some animals eat other animals. Many animals eat both plants and animals. Most people eat both plants and animals.

▶ **CLASSIFY** How do plants get food?

▲ **This heron is eating a fish.**

Food Chain

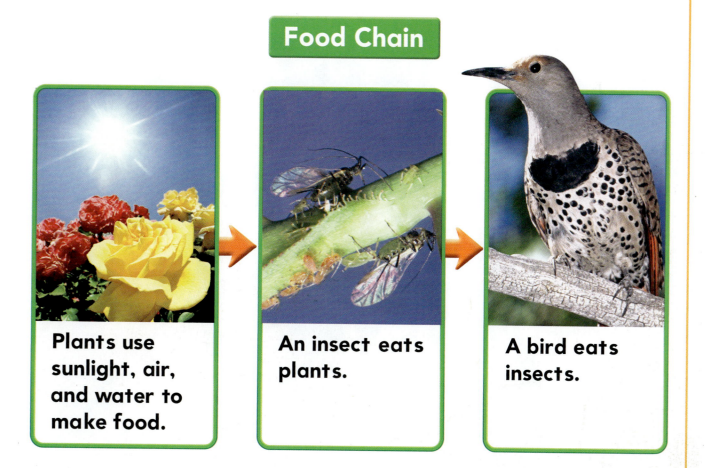

Plants use sunlight, air, and water to make food.

An insect eats plants.

A bird eats insects.

Water, Air, and Space

Plants and animals need water, air, and space to live. Most plants get water from the ground. Many animals get water by drinking. Some animals get water from the food they eat.

Plants need water to live.

How are the giraffes getting what they need?

Living things need air and space to live and grow. Plants use air to help them make food. Animals breathe in air.

Plants need space so that they can get the sunlight and water they need. Animals need space so that they can find food and homes.

Plants need space to grow.

▶ **CLASSIFY** How do animals get water?

Whales breathe air just as you do.

Shelter

Animals need shelter. **Shelter** is a safe place for animals to live. Animals find shelter in trees, in mud, and under the ground. Some animals even find shelter on other animals.

shelter in the ground

shelter on another animal

Lesson Wrap-Up

1. **Vocabulary** What kinds of **food** do animals eat?

2. **Reading Skill** What do plants need to live?

3. **Observe** Look at the picture. What need is the child taking care of?

Technology Visit www.eduplace.com/scp/ to find out more about the needs of living things.

LINKS for Home and School

Math — Measure Living Things

Use a ruler to measure a plant. Record your data in a table. Measure again every month. Tell how much the plant grew.

Measurements of My Plants	
Date	Measurement
October 1	3 inches
November 1	4 inches
December 1	$4\frac{1}{2}$ inches
January 1	5 inches
February 1	6 inches

Social Studies — Where People Live

Draw a picture of a place where people live. Write a sentence to tell how the place meets people's needs.

It keeps people warm.

Chapter 4 Review and Test Prep

Visual Summary

The world is made of living and nonliving things.

Living Thing	Nonliving Thing
• grows and changes • makes other living things like itself • needs food, water, air, and space	• does not eat, drink and grow • does not make other things like itself • does not need food, water, and air

Main Ideas

1. What do all living things need? (p. B8)

2. How are nonliving things different from living things? (p. B10)

3. How do plants use sunlight? (pp. B16–B17)

4. Where do most plants get water? (p. B18)

SAT 10 Practice

Vocabulary and Science Skills

Choose the correct answer.

5. A living thing needs _____.
   ○ trees   ○ fire   ○ water

6. Plants need sunlight to make _____.
   ○ food   ○ space   ○ seeds

7. Which is a nonliving thing?
   ○ flower   ○ book   ○ bird

8. A safe place for animals is _____.
   ○ a shelter   ○ a park   ○ a street

9. All living things _____.
   ○ sleep   ○ grow   ○ run

10. Shelter for a fox might be in _____.
   ○ the ground   ○ a pond
   ○ some mud

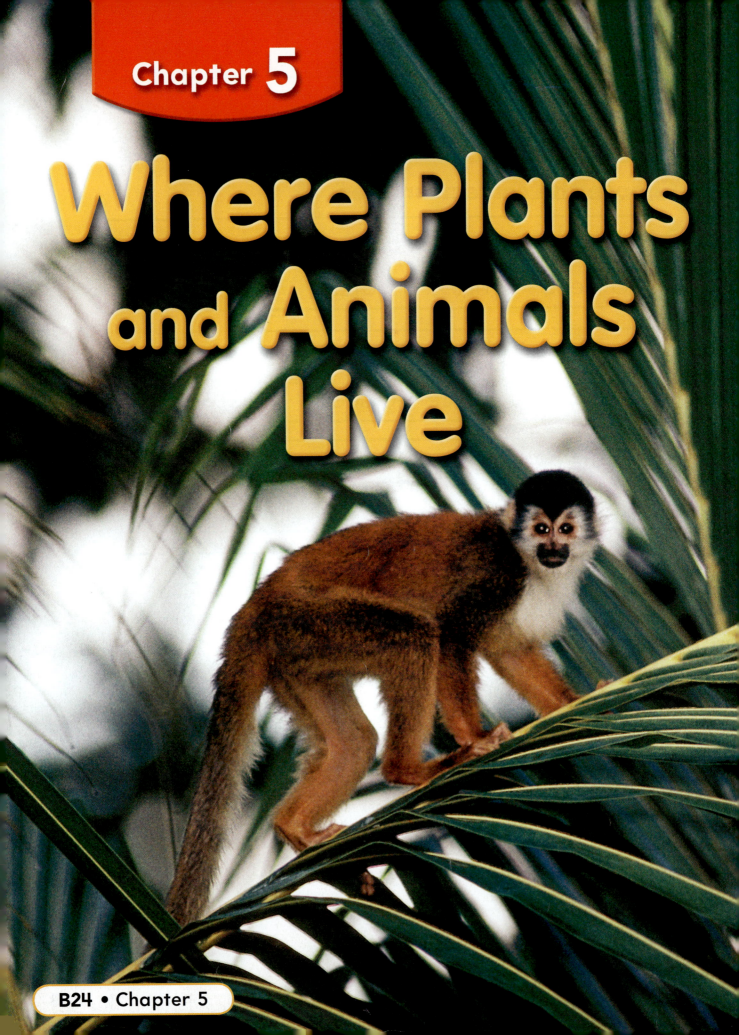

Chapter 5

Where Plants and Animals Live

Vocabulary Preview

forest
ocean
wetland
desert

forest
A forest is a place with many trees that grow close together.

ocean
An ocean is a large body of salty water.

wetland
A wetland is a low area of land that is very wet.

desert
A desert is a place with very little water.

Lesson 1

What Lives in Forests?

Science and You
You save the home of many living things when you protect a tree.

Inquiry Skill
Communicate Share information with others.

What You Need

hand lens

crayons

paper

Investigate

Observe a Tree

Steps

1. **Observe** Go outside. Use a hand lens to look closely at the parts of a tree.

2. **Record Data** Make a list of living things you find. Then draw a tree. Show the living things that you found.

3. **Communicate** Talk about your drawing with a partner. Find out if you saw different things.

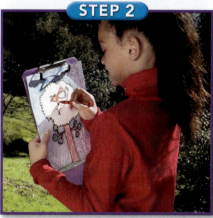

Think and Share

1. What did you find on and under the tree?
2. **Infer** How do trees help the living things you saw?

Investigate More!

Work Together Work with a partner. Talk about what should be in a forest. Choose the best ideas. Then make a model of a forest in a shoebox.

Learn by Reading

Vocabulary
forest

Reading Skill
Main Idea and Details

A Forest

A **forest** is a place with many trees that grow close together. Forest animals live in trees, bushes, or on the forest floor. Animals use the living and nonliving things in a forest for food and shelter.

▶ **MAIN IDEA** What is a forest?

What are some living and nonliving things in the forest?

bear

snake

katydid

Other Kinds of Forests

There are many kinds of forests. Some forests are hot and rainy. Others are cold and dry. There are different kinds of plants and animals in each kind of forest.

🔸 **MAIN IDEA** How are forests different from one another?

▲ great horned owl

◀ bobcat

A pine forest can be warm or cold. It is not as wet as a rain forest.

It is warm and rainy in a tropical rain forest.

parrot ▶

Lesson Wrap-Up

1. **Vocabulary** What do you call a place that has many trees close together?

2. **Reading Skill** Are all forests the same? Tell why or why not.

3. **Communicate** Tell a partner what a tropical rain forest is like.

Technology Visit www.eduplace.com/scp/ to find out more about forests.

Lesson 2

What Lives in Oceans and Wetlands?

Science and You
You can have fun playing in the ocean, but it is also a home for many living things.

Inquiry Skill
Compare Tell how objects or events are alike or different.

What You Need

animal pictures

Investigate

Compare Animals

Steps

1. **Compare** Look at animal pictures. Tell how animals are alike and different.

2. **Classify** Sort the animal pictures into groups that are alike in one way.

3. Name your groups. Make a list of the animals in each group.

STEP 1

STEP 2

STEP 3

Think and Share

1. **Compare** Tell what is alike about the animals in each group. Tell how the groups are different.

2. What body parts do you think help these animals live where they do?

Investigate More!

Ask Questions Make a list of things you want to learn about one animal. Write each thing as a question. Make a plan to answer your questions.

Learn by Reading

The Ocean

Vocabulary
ocean
wetland

Reading Skill
Compare and Contrast

An **ocean** is a large body of salty water. Oceans are nonliving things, but they have many living things in them. Some animals live on land but eat ocean animals. Other animals live in the air and water near the shore. Many animals live in deep water.

What are some living and nonliving things in the ocean?

whale

jellyfish

manta

Ocean animals have parts that help them stay alive in water. Fish have fins and tails to swim. They have gills to breathe air. Some animals have colors that help them hide.

▶ **COMPARE AND CONTRAST** What are some ways in which fish are alike?

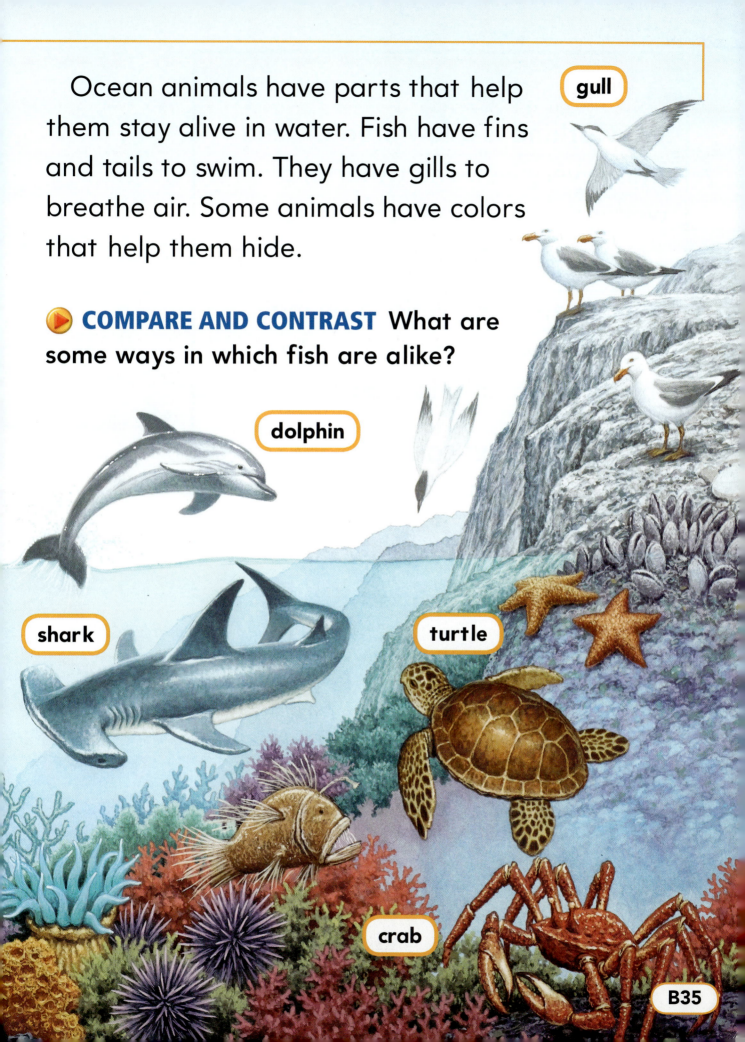

A Wetland

A **wetland** is a low area of land that is very wet. The water in a wetland can be salty or not salty.

Many kinds of plants and animals live in wetlands. Wetland animals find food, water, and shelter in the mud, water, and plants.

▶ **COMPARE AND CONTRAST** What are two different kinds of wetlands?

Lesson Wrap-Up

1. **Vocabulary** What is a large body of salty water called?

2. **Reading Skill** How are oceans different from wetlands?

3. **Compare** How are oceans like wetlands?

Technology Visit www.eduplace.com/scp/ to find out more about oceans and wetlands.

Focus On Biography

Marjory Stoneman Douglas

Writer and Environmentalist

Marjory Douglas worried about the Everglades. The Everglades is a Florida wetland.

People wanted to build homes, stores, and roads in the Everglades. Douglas knew that would cause many plants and animals to die. So she wrote books and stories to tell why the Everglades should be saved.

Her work paid off. Today the Everglades is a national park. It will be protected forever.

SOCIAL STUDIES LINK

sawgrass

purple gallinule

Sharing Ideas

1. **Write About It** Why did Douglas worry about the Everglades?

2. **Talk About It** Use your own words to tell why people remember Marjory Stoneman Douglas.

Lesson 3

What Lives in a Desert?

Science and You
You need to drink a lot of water when you are in a desert.

Inquiry Skill
Use Numbers You can count to know the right amount each time.

What You Need

dry sponges

wax paper

dropper and water

plate

Investigate

Wet or Dry

Steps

1. **Use Numbers** Squeeze four droppers full of water onto a sponge. Put four droppers of water on the other sponge.

2. Wrap wax paper all around one sponge. Do not wrap the other sponge.

3. **Compare** Put the sponges on a plate. Wait one day. Touch the sponges. How are they different?

Think and Share

1. Which sponge was wetter?
2. **Infer** What can you say about the wax paper and water?

Investigate More!

Experiment Repeat the experiment two more times exactly the same way. What happens? What does this tell you about science experiments?

Learn by Reading

▶ **Vocabulary**
desert

▶ **Reading Skill**
Draw Conclusions

The Desert

A **desert** is a place with very little water. The air can be hot or cold. The ground in a hot desert is mostly covered with rocks or sand.

Living in a desert is not easy. It can be hard to find food and water in such a dry place.

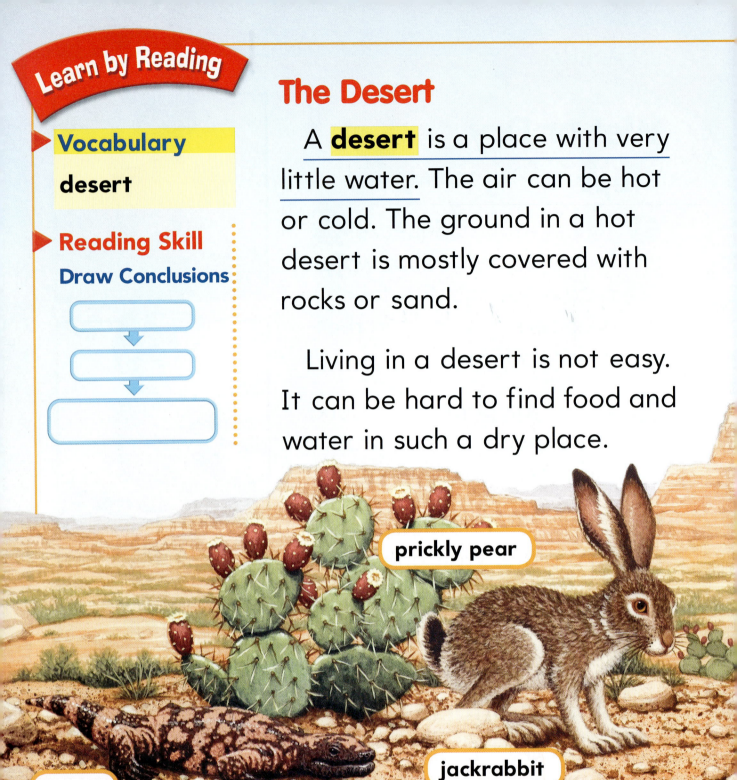

prickly pear

lizard

jackrabbit

rat

What are some living and nonliving things in the desert?

The air is hot in this desert. Many animals hide or sleep during the day. They look for food at night when the air is cool.

▶ **DRAW CONCLUSIONS** Why do many desert animals sleep during the day?

Living in Deserts

Desert plants and animals have parts that help them live in dry places. A cactus has thick stems and waxy skin that hold water. A kangaroo rat's body makes water from the seeds it eats.

A camel has wide feet that help it walk in sand. ▶

Lesson Wrap-Up

1. **Vocabulary** What is a place with very little water called?

2. **Reading Skill** Why do many desert plants have waxy skin?

3. **Use Numbers** How can you use numbers to help you do a science experiment?

🖥 **Technology** Visit www.eduplace.com/scp/ to find out more about deserts.

LINKS for Home and School

Math Make a Counting Book

Make a counting book. On the first page, draw one living thing. Write the number 1 on the page. Make seven more pages. Add one living thing each time.

1. How many things are on your last page?
2. How many more things are on the third page than the first page?

Language Arts What If?

What if the whole world was a wetland? What if animals only lived in deserts? Think of a "what if" question. Then write a story to answer the question.

Chapter 5 Review and Test Prep

Visual Summary

Living things are found in many places.

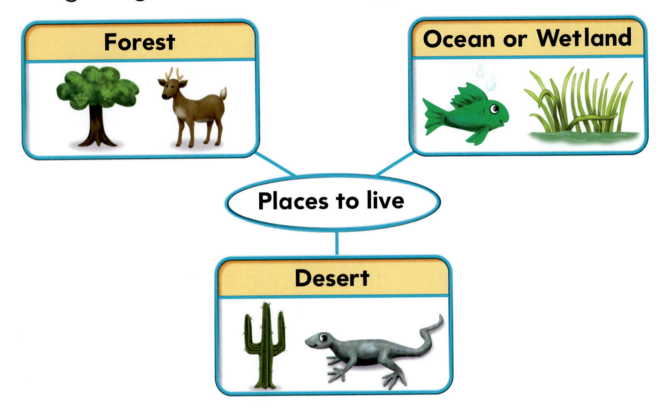

Main Ideas

1. What are two kinds of forests? (pp. B30–B31)

2. Name three animals that live in an ocean. (pp. B34–B35)

3. Where do wetland animals find food, water, and shelter? (p. B36)

4. What helps a cactus hold water? (p. B44)

SAT 10 Practice

Vocabulary and Science Skills

Choose the correct answer.

5. Many trees grow in ____.
   ○ a desert   ○ a forest   ○ an ocean

6. Where might alligators live?
   ○ a desert   ○ a forest   ○ a wetland

7. Which lives in an ocean?
   ○ whale   ○ rabbit   ○ bear

8. Deserts have only a little ____.
   ○ sand   ○ water   ○ air

9. A desert cactus holds water in its ____.
   ○ stem   ○ flowers   ○ spines

10. Which helps fish swim in oceans?
    ○ sand   ○ colors   ○ fins

UNIT B Wrap-Up

Discover!

Why do you find shells on the beach?

Some ocean animals are covered with a hard shell. The hard shell protects the animal's soft body. After the animal dies, the shell is empty. Waves push the empty shell onto the beach.

Go to **www.eduplace.com/scp/** to visit the underwater world of shells.

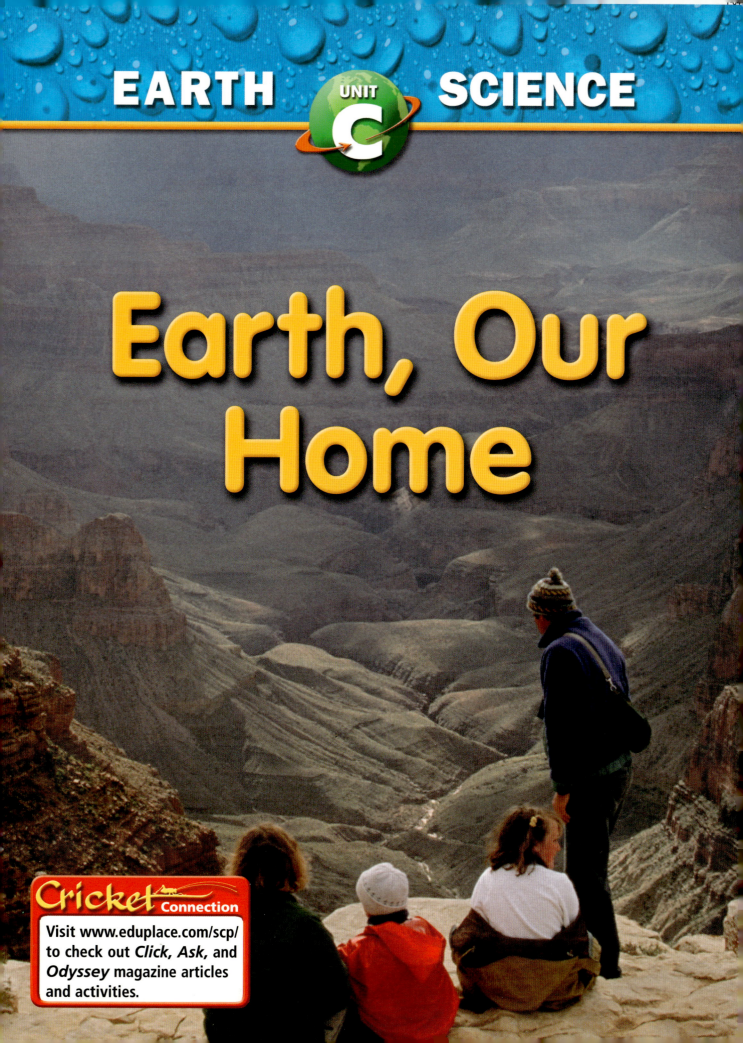

EARTH SCIENCE
UNIT C

Earth, Our Home

Reading in Science............. C2

Chapter 6
Looking at Our Earth C4

Chapter 7
Caring for Our Earth C30

Independent Reading

7 Uses for Air

What Makes a Garden Grow

We Can Recycle

Discover!

Why do rocks have different colors?

Think about this question as you read. You will have the answer by the end of the unit.

Dirt

by Steve Tomecek
illustrated by Nancy Woodman

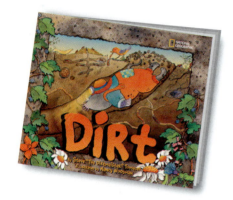

C2 • Unit C

Some people think that dirt is just something to be cleaned up—like the stuff you wash out of your clothes. But dirt is really one of the most important things on earth.

Reading in Science

Strategy: Summarize

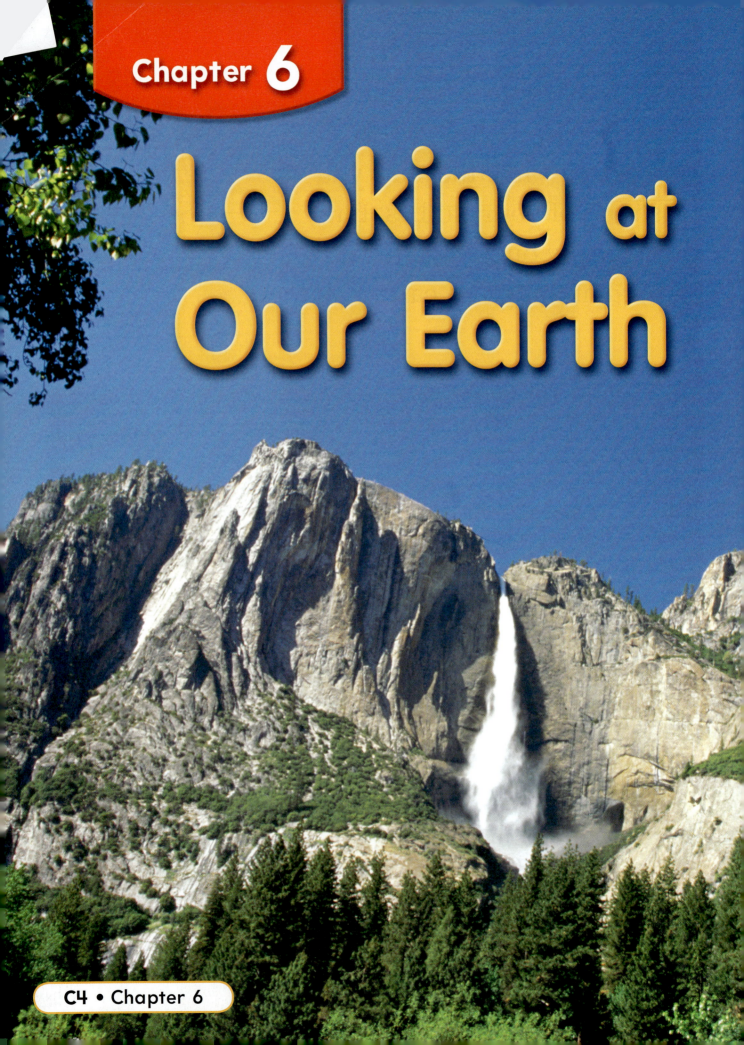

Chapter 6
Looking at Our Earth

C4 • Chapter 6

Vocabulary Preview

natural resource
mineral
boulders
soil
humus

natural resource
A natural resource is something from Earth that people use.

mineral
A mineral is a nonliving thing found in nature.

soil
Soil is the loose top layer of Earth.

humus
Humus is bits of rotting plants and animals in soil.

Lesson 1

What Covers Earth?

Science and You
You need fresh water to live and grow.

Inquiry Skill
Use Numbers You can count things to find out how amounts are alike or different.

What You Need

map

counters

paper and marker

Investigate

Land and Water

Steps

1. Use green counters to cover all the land on the map. Use blue counters to cover all the water.

2. **Classify** Sort the counters into two groups called **Land** and **Water**.

3. **Use Numbers** Count each group of counters. Record your data.

STEP 1

STEP 2

STEP 3

Think and Share

1. **Use Data** Did more counters cover land or water?

2. **Infer** Why do you think Earth is called the water planet?

Investigate More!

Work Together Work with your classmates. Find or draw pictures of things that live on land, in water, or in the air. Explain what your pictures show.

Learn by Reading

Vocabulary

natural resource

Reading Skill

Compare and Contrast

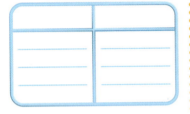

Water Resources

A **natural resource** is something from Earth that people use. Air and land are both natural resources. Water is a natural resource, too. Water covers most of Earth.

People use water in many ways. They swim and play in it. They travel on it. They wash and clean with it.

river

ocean

Ocean water is salty. Fresh water is not salty. Fresh water is found in streams, rivers, lakes, and the ground. People need fresh water to drink.

▶ **COMPARE AND CONTRAST** How is lake water different from ocean water?

Land and Air Resources

Earth's land and air are natural resources. People use soil to grow plants. They use trees to make paper, furniture, and buildings.

People use rocks to make statues and buildings. They melt sand to make glass.

Air is a natural resource that living things need. You cannot see air, but you use it every time you breathe.

▶ **COMPARE AND CONTRAST** How do people use land and air resources?

Lesson Wrap-Up

1. **Vocabulary** What do you call something from Earth that people use?

2. **Reading Skill** How are water and land resources alike? How are they different?

3. **Use Numbers** What are four objects that are made from plants?

Technology Visit www.eduplace.com/scp/ to find out more about natural resources.

Lesson 2

How Do People Use Rocks and Minerals?

Science and You
People use rocks to make statues and buildings.

Inquiry Skill
Experiment Make a plan to collect data and then communicate the results.

What You Need

rocks

hand lens

sorting mat

Investigate

Compare Rocks

Steps

1. **Observe** Use a hand lens to look at each rock. Touch each rock.

2. **Compare** Look for ways in which the rocks are alike. Look for ways in which the rocks are different.

3. **Classify** Sort the rocks into groups. Tell how the rocks in a group are alike.

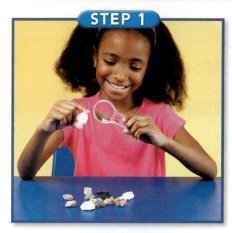

STEP 1

STEP 2

STEP 3

Think and Share

1. **Communicate** Tell what you learned about the rocks you observed.

2. What are some other ways to sort the rocks?

Investigate More!

Experiment Rub each rock on different materials, such as the back of a tile. Talk with others about what you observe.

C13

Learn by Reading

Vocabulary
mineral
boulders

Reading Skill
Main Idea and Details

Rocks and Minerals

A **mineral** is a nonliving thing found in nature. A rock is a nonliving thing made of one or more minerals. Rocks and minerals are natural resources.

Different rocks have different minerals in them. That is why they are different colors.

Minerals

▼ amethyst in a geode

▼ cinnabar

gypsum ▶

Rocks come in many sizes. Some mountains are made of rock. Very large rocks are sometimes called **boulders**. Sand is made of very small rocks or minerals.

▲ sandstone

▶ **MAIN IDEA** What are rocks made of?

Rocks

granite ▲

limestone ▶

◀ obsidian

◀ A conglomerate is made of bits of different rocks.

C15

Using Rocks and Minerals

People use rocks and minerals in different ways. Talc, graphite, and gold are some of the softest minerals. People use them for powder, pencils, and medals. Garnet is harder than graphite. People use garnets for jewelry.

graphite

garnet

gold

talc

People use hard rocks for buildings, statues, and bridges. Limestone, sandstone, and granite are hard rocks.

▶ **MAIN IDEA** What are some ways that people use rocks and minerals?

limestone

▲ Chicago Water Tower

Lesson Wrap-Up

1. **Vocabulary** What is a **mineral**?

2. **Reading Skill** Tell three things you know about rocks and minerals.

3. **Experiment** How can experimenting with rocks help you learn about them?

Technology Visit www.eduplace.com/scp/ to find out more about rocks and minerals.

C17

Focus On

Readers' Theater

Rock Stars

Cast
Narrator
Paul: a sculptor
Susan: a jeweler
Art: a builder
Jon: a road worker
Carla: a miner

C18 • Chapter 6

READING LINK

Narrator: People use rocks in many ways. Some jobs depend on rocks.

Paul: I am a sculptor. I carve rocks to make art.

Carla: What kind of rocks do you use?

Paul: I use marble. Marble is a pretty rock. It is very strong, too.

Art: I am a builder. I use rocks that are hard and pretty, too! I like sandstone and granite.

Susan: What do you use them for?

Art: I cut and polish rocks to make blocks and tiles. I use the blocks and tiles in buildings.

Susan: I am a jeweler. I cut and polish pretty rocks, too. I use them to make jewelry.

Jon: I am a road worker. I use crushed rocks, like limestone, to make concrete to build roads.

Carla: Very interesting. But you would not have jobs without me!

Paul, Susan, Art, and Jon: Why?

Carla: I am a miner. I dig up rocks from the ground. Then people like you can use them!

Paul, Susan, Art, and Jon: Thanks Carla! You rock!

Sharing Ideas

1. **Write About It** Glass is made from melted sand. Write a story telling how a glassmaker is a rock star.
2. **Talk About It** What would your life be like without rocks?

Lesson 3

What Is Soil?

Science and You
You may think that soil is just dirt, but it is an important natural resource.

Inquiry Skill
Observe Use your senses to learn about soil.

What You Need

goggles

soil

toothpick

hand lens

Investigate

Observe Soil

Steps

1. **Observe** Spread apart the bits of soil. Look at the soil with a hand lens. Record what you see.
Safety: Wear goggles!

2. Squeeze a handful of soil. Slowly open your hand. Record what happens.

3. Rub some soil between your hands. Tell how the soil feels. **Safety:** Wash your hands!

STEP 1

STEP 2

STEP 3

Think and Share

1. What do you think soil is made of?
2. **Infer** Why do you think the soil stuck together?

Investigate More!

Experiment Find out about other kinds of soil. With an adult, dig soil from two different places. Compare the small parts in each kind of soil.

Learn by Reading

Vocabulary
soil
humus

Reading Skill
Cause and Effect

Soil

Soil is the loose top layer of Earth. Soil is made of bits of minerals and rock, rotting plants, and rotting animals. The bits of rotting plants and animals are called **humus**. The rocks, minerals, and humus help plants grow. Some water and air are also found in soil.

Kinds of Soil

Topsoil	Clay Soil	Sandy Soil
• black or brown • best for plant growth	• brown, red, or yellow • sticky when wet	• tan or light brown • holds little water

Soil is a natural resource. Most plants need soil to grow. Many animals live in soil. They help the soil by digging in it and breaking it into small pieces. This keeps air in the soil. It makes space for water to get into the soil, too.

▶ **CAUSE AND EFFECT** How do animals help soil?

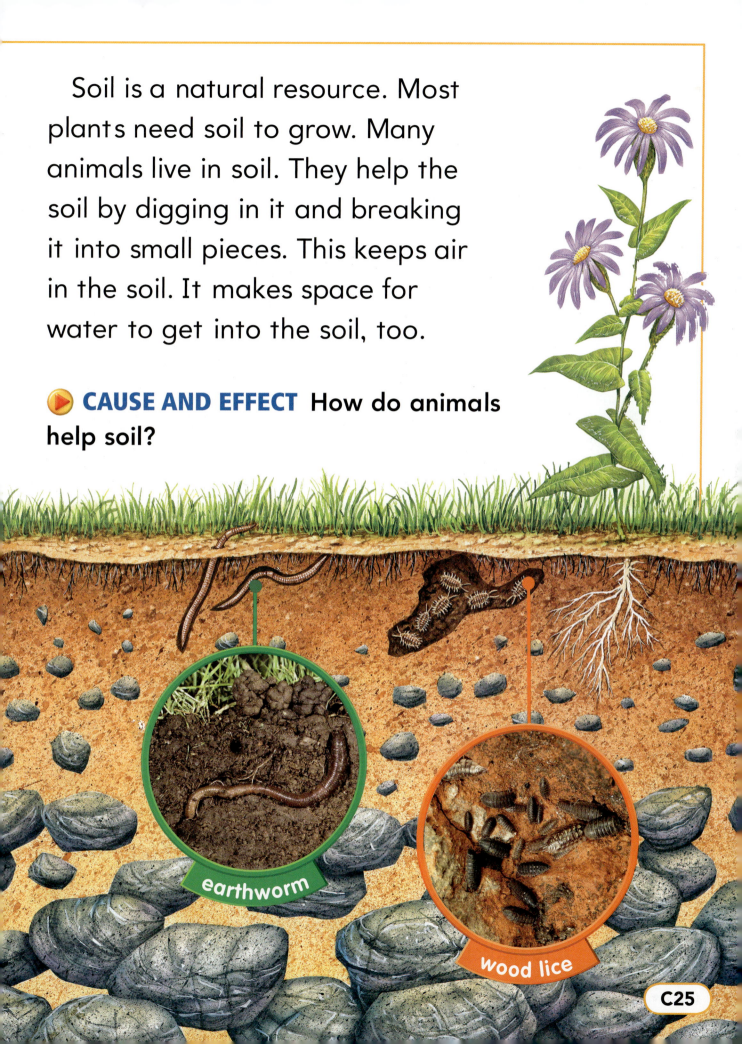

earthworm

wood lice

Saving Soil

It is important to save soil because it takes a long time for soil to form. Water and wind can take soil away. One way to save soil is to grow plants. The plant roots help hold soil in place.

soil with plants

soil without plants

Lesson Wrap-Up

1. **Vocabulary** What is **soil**?
2. **Reading Skill** What causes soil to go away?
3. **Observe** What can you learn about soil by observing it?

Technology Visit www.eduplace.com/scp/ to find out more about soil.

LINKS for Home and School

Math **Make a Pictograph**

Take a class survey. Count the number of children whose families grow flowers, vegetables, or houseplants. Record your data in a pictograph.

How We Use Soil	
To Grow Flowers	☺☺☺☺☺☺☺☺☺☺
To Grow Vegetables	☺☺☺☺☺☺
To Grow Houseplants	☺☺☺☺

Each ☺ stands for 1 child.

Music **This Land Is Your Land**

Sing "This Land Is Your Land." Then draw a picture to show how people use the land where you live.

Chapter 6 Review and Test Prep

Visual Summary

Earth has many natural resources.

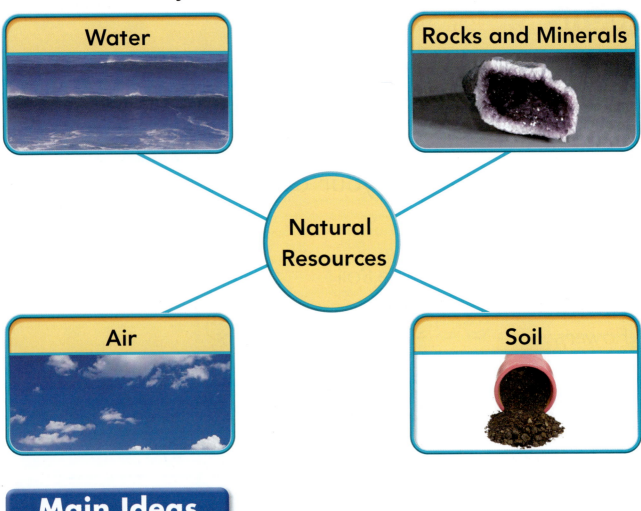

Main Ideas

1. Why is water a natural resource? (pp. C8–C9)

2. Name three resources from land. (pp. C10–C11)

3. What are two things that people use rocks and minerals for? (pp. C16–C17)

4. What is soil made of? (p. C24)

SAT 10 Practice

Vocabulary and Science Skills

Choose the correct answer.

5. Bits of rotting plants and animals in soil is called ____.
   ○ rock   ○ humus   ○ minerals

6. Which is a natural resource?
   ○ glass   ○ air   ○ sandwich

7. Which is made of very small rocks?
   ○ sand   ○ mountains   ○ boulders

8. Rocks are made of one or more ____.
   ○ mountains   ○ animals   ○ minerals

9. Which can help save soil?
   ○ plants   ○ water   ○ wind

10. Which is made from trees?
   ○ paper   ○ crayon   ○ chalk

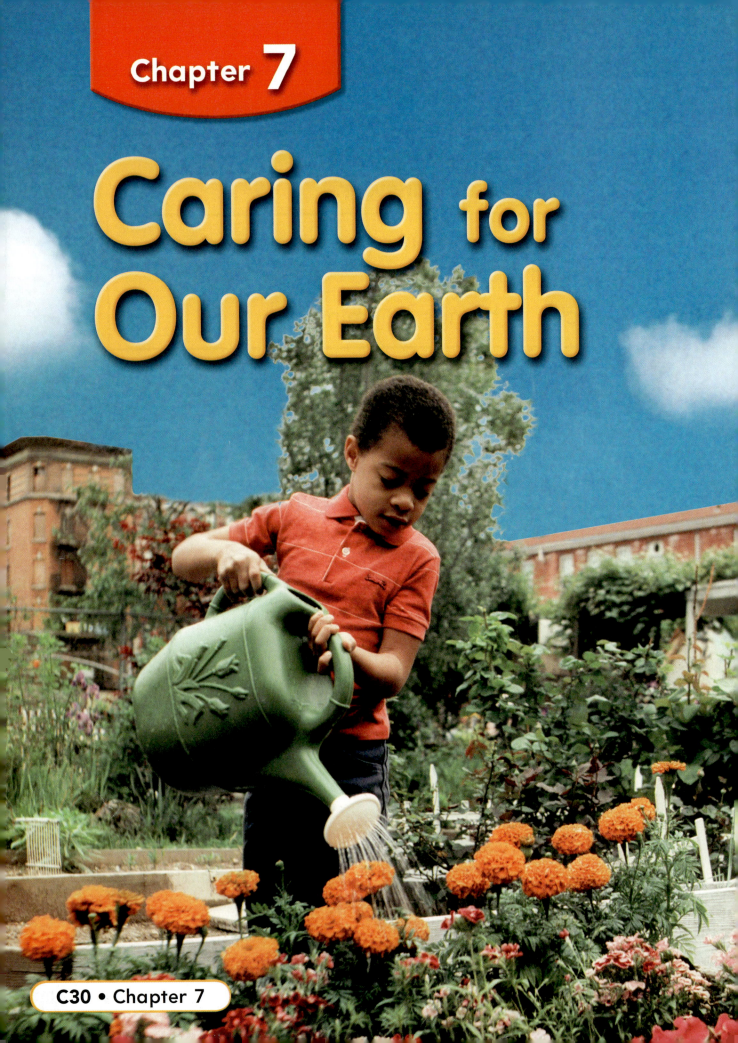

Vocabulary Preview

air pollution
water pollution
reuse
recycle
reduce

air pollution
Air pollution happens when harmful things get into air.

water pollution
Water pollution happens when harmful things get into water.

reuse
Reuse means to use something again.

recycle
When you recycle an object, a factory takes it and makes a new object from it.

Lesson 1

How Do We Use Air?

Science and You
You use air every time you breathe.

Inquiry Skill
Use Data You can use what you observe and record to learn more about something.

What You Need

petroleum jelly

2 index cards

hand lens

Investigate

Collect Pollution

Steps

1. Spread petroleum jelly on two index cards.

2. Place one card outdoors. Place the other card indoors.

3. **Observe** Wait three days. Then use a hand lens to look at the cards.

4. **Record Data** Draw or write what you see.

STEP 1

STEP 2

STEP 3

Think and Share

1. **Infer** Where did the dust and dirt come from?

2. **Use Data** Compare the two cards. Which card has more dust and dirt? Tell why.

Investigate More!

Experiment Repeat the experiment two more times. Predict what will happen. Then tell why you think the results were the same or different each time.

C33

Learn by Reading

Vocabulary
air pollution

Reading Skill
Draw Conclusions

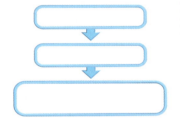

Air

Air is a natural resource. People, plants, and animals need air to stay alive. You cannot see air, but you can feel it push against you. Sometimes you can smell things in the air.

▼ The boy blows air into the bubbles.

People use air in many ways. A sailboat uses air to move across the water. You can use air to cool off on a hot day. Moving air can help make electricity to run things like TVs and lamps.

▶ **DRAW CONCLUSIONS** Why is air important?

▲ **Windmills help make electricity.**

Air pushes on the sail.

Air Pollution

Air pollution happens when harmful things get into air. Dust and smoke from cars, fires, and factories are pollution. They can make air harmful to breathe. Pollution can make living things sick.

air pollution

clean air

Clean air helps plants grow and stay green. It helps animals and people have healthy lungs. Clean air also keeps buildings and statues clean.

▶ **DRAW CONCLUSIONS**
Why is it important to keep air clean?

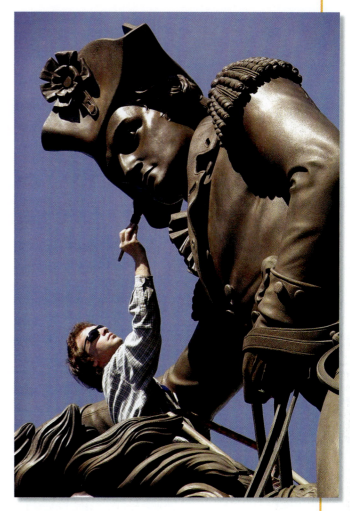

Pollution is being cleaned off.

Lesson Wrap-Up

1. **Vocabulary** What causes **air pollution**?
2. **Reading Skill** Why does a fire cause air pollution?
3. **Use Data** If you find bits of dirt on a windowsill, what do you know about the air?

Technology Visit www.eduplace.com/scp/ to find out more about air.

Lesson 2

How Do We Use Water?

Science and You
When you ride in a boat you are using water.

Inquiry Skill
Use Models Use something like a real thing to learn how the real thing works.

What You Need

wire

self-stick notes

spool

water

tub

Investigate

A Waterwheel

Steps

1. Put self-stick notes on the edges of a spool.

STEP 1

2. Put wire through the spool to make a waterwheel.
Safety: Use wire carefully!

STEP 2

3. **Use Models** Hold the waterwheel over a tub. Slowly pour water over a side of the waterwheel. Record what happens.

STEP 3

Think and Share

1. **Communicate** Tell what happened to the spool.
2. **Infer** What made the spool turn?

Investigate More!

Experiment Make a waterwheel that turns faster. Use objects such as clay, cardboard, and tape. Share your results.

Learn by Reading

Vocabulary
water pollution

Reading Skill
Categorize and Classify

Water

Water is found in lakes, rivers, oceans, and under the ground. Water is a natural resource that you cannot live without.

You use water every day. You drink water. You use water when you take a bath. You use it when you swim, cook, clean, and water plants.

drinking ▶

◀ washing

People use water to put out fires. They use water in lakes, rivers, and oceans when they fish, swim, or travel. People also use moving water to make electricity.

▶ **CLASSIFY** What are three ways people use water?

▲ having fun

▲ fighting fires

▲ Water in a dam is used to make electricity.

Water Pollution

Water pollution happens when harmful things get into water. Putting trash and oil in water causes water pollution. Polluted water can kill plants. It can make animals and people sick if they drink or swim in it.

cleaning an oil-covered bird

oil slick

People can help clean up pollution. They can pick up trash. They can clean up oil. They can stop putting harmful things into the water, too!

🔴 **CLASSIFY** How can people clean up water pollution?

Lesson Wrap-Up

① **Vocabulary** What happens when harmful things get into water?

② **Reading Skill** What are two things that cause water pollution?

③ **Use Models** How can using a model help you learn about water and its uses?

🪣 **Technology** Visit www.eduplace.com/scp/ to find out more about water.

Focus On: Health and Safety

Water Safety

You can have lots of fun in water. You can play or swim in water. You can ride in boats on water. Having a good time means having a safe time. Here are some ways to stay safe in water.

1 Learn to swim. This is the most important rule for water safety. You should learn to float, too.

READING LINK

2 **Always have an adult with you.** An adult can tell you where it is safe to swim or ride in a boat.

3 **Follow the rules.** Always walk near a pool. Stay out of the water in bad weather.

4 **Wear a life jacket on a boat.** Everyone on a boat should have a life jacket.

5 **Come out of the water if you are tired or cold.** Accidents can happen if you are tired or cold.

Sharing Ideas

1. **Write About It** How can following rules help you stay safe near water?
2. **Talk About It** Why is swimming the most important rule for water safety?

C45

Lesson 3

How Can We Help Earth?

Science and You
You can help Earth by recycling cans, bottles, and paper.

Inquiry Skill
Classify Group things that are alike in some way.

What You Need

trash objects

index cards

marker

Investigate

Sort Your Trash

Steps

1. **Classify** Think about what each object is made of. Sort objects into groups.

2. **Record Data** Put an index card next to each group. Write a name for the group on each card.

3. Write on each card three ways you could reuse objects in that group.

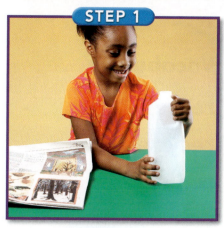

STEP 1

STEP 2

STEP 3

Think and Share

1. **Compare** How are the objects in each group alike?

2. **Infer** Why might it be a good idea to use some trash again?

Investigate More!

Solve a Problem How much paper does your class throw away in one week? Collect the paper in a trash bag. Then think of ways to save paper.

C47

Learn by Reading

Vocabulary
reuse
recycle
reduce

Reading Skill
Sequence

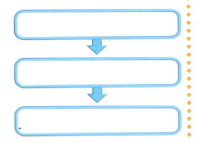

Reuse

Earth's natural resources may not last forever. You can save resources if you reuse, recycle, and reduce trash.

When you **reuse**, you use something again. This means that resources are not used to make a new thing.

▼ tire swing and tire sandals

▲ pencil holder

Watts Towers reuse tiles, metal, and glass. ▶

Think about how you can reuse something before you throw it away. Use a milk carton to plant flowers. Use pictures in old magazines to make cards. Reusing can help natural resources last longer.

⏵ **SEQUENCE** What should you think about before you throw something away?

▲ license-plate purse

C49

Recycle

When you **recycle** an object, a factory takes it and makes a new object from it. People recycle newspapers, paper, plastic, and cans. They also recycle glass, rubber, batteries, and cardboard.

plastic bottles   backpack

newspapers   box

First, things go to recycling centers. Second, factories make the recycled things into resources again. Third, the resources are made into new things that you can use.

▶ **SEQUENCE** What happens when things are recycled?

old cans

new cans

old sneaker

running track

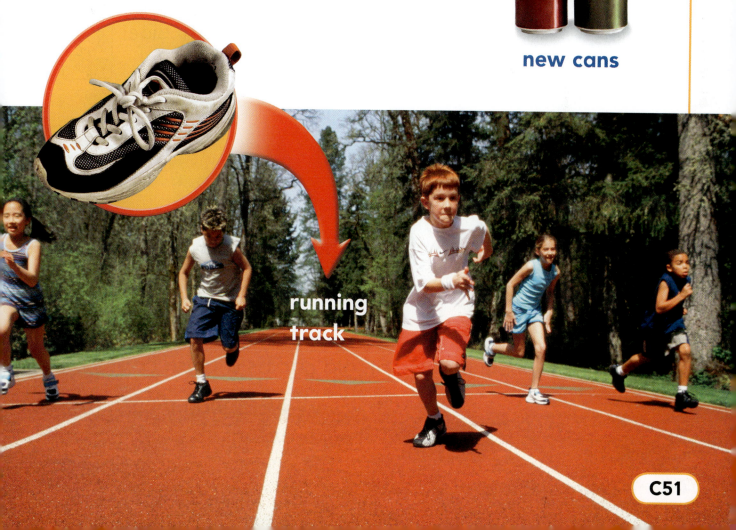

Reduce

When you **reduce**, you use less of something. Try to use up old crayons before you get new ones. Take care of your things so that they last longer.

The picture shows other ways you can reduce what you use.

1. **Vocabulary** What does it mean to **recycle**?

2. **Reading Skill** List the steps in recycling.

3. **Classify** Do you reuse, recycle, or reduce when you use an old can as a trash can?

Technology Visit www.eduplace.com/scp/ to find out more about recycling.

LINKS for Home and School

Math Sort and Count Plastic

Collect and wash all the plastic bottles you use in five days. Look for a number on the bottom of each bottle. Make a chart to record what you find.

Kinds of Plastic Bottles	
Kind	Number
Number 1	7
Number 2	4
Number 3	1

Write a number sentence to show how many number 1 and number 2 bottles you have.

Social Studies Keep It Clean

Everyone can help keep air, land, and water clean. Make a poster to remind people to clean up after themselves.

Chapter 7 Review and Test Prep

Visual Summary

There are many ways to care for Earth.

| Keep air, water, and land clean | Reuse | Recycle | Reduce |

Main Ideas

1. What are two ways that people use air? (pp. C34–C35)

2. What are three ways that people use water? (pp. C40–C41)

3. Why is water pollution harmful? (p. C42)

4. What happens when you reduce? (p. C52)

SAT 10 Practice

Vocabulary and Science Skills

Choose the correct answer.

5. Using an old tire as a swing is _____.
○ reducing   ○ recycling   ○ reusing

6. Which can cause air pollution?
○ smoke   ○ trash   ○ trees

7. Which means to use less of something?
○ reduce   ○ recycle   ○ reuse

8. Which can cause water pollution?
○ birds   ○ oil   ○ plants

9. Which do you save when you use both sides of paper?
○ natural resource   ○ can   ○ bottle

10. People use air when they _____.
○ breathe   ○ cook   ○ drink

Wrap-Up

Discover!

Why do rocks have different colors?

Rocks are made of one or more minerals. Minerals are different colors because of the way they are formed. The color of a rock depends on the minerals inside the rock.

Go to **www.eduplace.com/scp/** to see rocks and their colors.

EARTH SCIENCE
UNIT D

Weather and the Sky

Reading in Science D2

Chapter 8
Weather and Seasons D4

Chapter 9
Changes in the Sky D42

Independent Reading

Time to Sleep

Measuring Weather

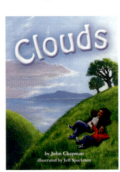
Clouds

What Will the Weather Be?

by Lynda DeWitt
illustrated by Carolyn Croll

D2 • Unit D

Weather forecasts tell us what kind of weather is coming. But predicting the weather is hard to do. It is easy to see what the weather is like right now. You can go outside and look.

Chapter 8
Weather and Seasons

Vocabulary Preview

weather
thermometer
temperature
water cycle
cloud
season
spring
summer
fall
winter

weather
Weather is what the air outside is like.

thermometer
A thermometer is a tool that measures temperature.

cloud
Many drops of water together form a cloud.

season
A season is a time of year that has its own kind of weather.

Lesson 1

What Is Weather?

Science and You
Observing the weather can help you decide to play inside or outside.

Inquiry Skill
Record Data You can use pictures to show what you observe.

What You Need

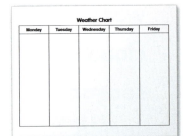
weather chart

weather pictures

scissors

glue

Investigate

Record Weather

Steps

1. **Observe** Look outside to see the weather today.

STEP 1

2. Cut out pictures that show the weather today. **Safety:** Scissors are sharp!

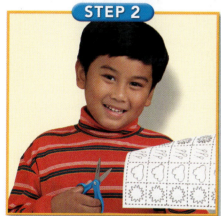
STEP 2

3. **Record Data** Glue the pictures in your weather chart.

4. Repeat each day for one week.

STEP 3

Think and Share

1. What does your chart tell you about the weather?
2. Why might you record two pictures for the same day?

Investigate More!

Work Together Record the weather for two more weeks. Talk with others. Were their data the same or different? Tell why.

D7

Learn by Reading

Vocabulary
weather

Reading Skill
Main Idea and Details

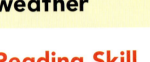

Kinds of Weather

Weather is what the air outside is like. There are many kinds of weather. Weather may be warm or cool. It may be rainy or sunny. It may be cloudy or windy.

How do you know it is warm and sunny here?

You can use your senses to observe the weather. You can see clouds. You can hear rain. You can feel warm or cool air. You can see wind move things.

▶ **MAIN IDEA** What are some kinds of weather?

▼ rainy

▲ windy and cloudy

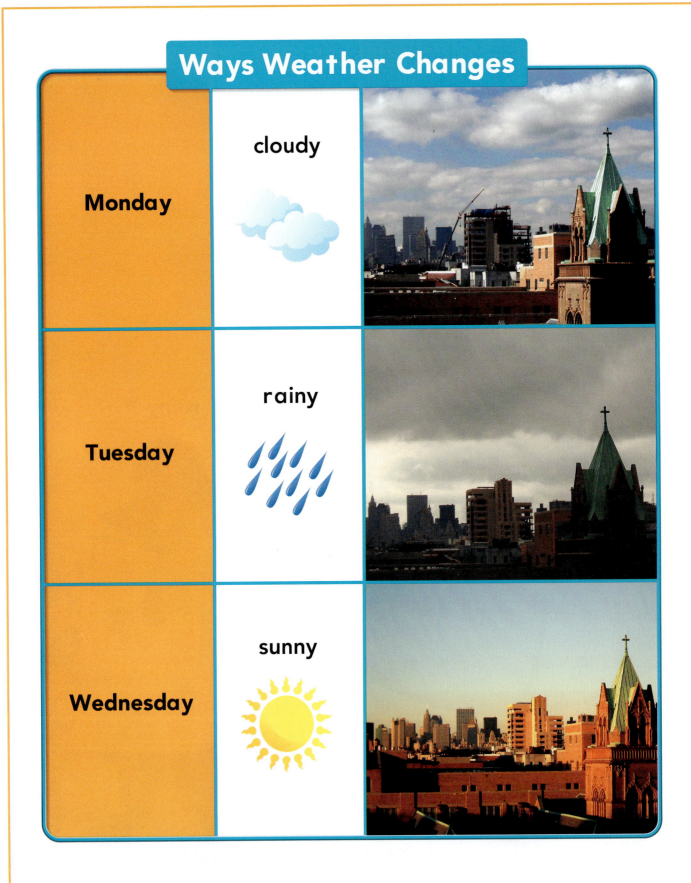

Weather Changes

Weather changes when the air changes. Weather can change from day to day. One day the weather can be sunny and warm. The next day it can be cloudy and cool. Then clouds may bring rain.

▶ **MAIN IDEA** How might weather change from day to day?

Lesson Wrap-Up

❶ **Vocabulary** Tell something that you know about **weather**.

❷ **Reading Skill** How can you use your senses to observe weather?

❸ **Record Data** Tell one way to record data.

🖥 **Technology** Visit www.eduplace.com/scp/ to find out more about weather.

D11

Lesson 2

How Can You Measure Weather?

Science and You
Reading a thermometer helps you know when you might need a jacket.

Inquiry Skill
Measure Use a tool to find how much or how many.

What You Need

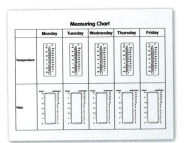
measuring chart

thermometer

ruler

rain collector

Investigate

Measure Weather

Steps

1. Take the thermometer and the rain collector outside.

2. **Record Data** Go outside again later. Read the thermometer. Record the temperature.

3. **Measure** Use a ruler to measure any rain. Record what you measure. Empty the rain collector.

4. Do these steps for five days.

Think and Share

1. How did tools help you learn about weather?
2. How did the weather change during the five days?

Investigate More!

Be an Inventor Invent a tool to show if wind is blowing. Try your tool. Explain how your tool works.

Learn by Reading

Vocabulary
thermometer
temperature

Reading Skill
Draw Conclusions

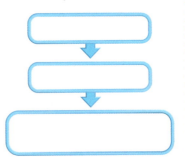

A Tool for Temperature

One way to tell about weather is to use tools. A **thermometer** is a tool that measures temperature. **Temperature** is how warm or cool something is.

What do these thermometers tell about the weather?

D14 • Chapter 8 • Lesson 2

Knowing the temperature helps you know what to wear. When the temperature is cold, you wear clothes that keep you warm. When it is hot, you wear clothes that keep you cool.

▶ **DRAW CONCLUSIONS** If you need a coat, what can you tell about the temperature?

Tools for Wind and Rain

You can use tools to measure wind and rain. A windsock and a wind vane show which way the wind blows. A windsock also shows how hard the wind blows. A rain gauge measures how much rain falls.

▶ **DRAW CONCLUSIONS** If a rain gauge is full, what can you tell about the weather?

▼ windsock

wind vane ▼

◀ rain gauge

Lesson Wrap-Up

❶ **Vocabulary** What is **temperature**?

❷ **Reading Skill** If a windsock is hanging down, what can you tell about the wind?

❸ **Measure** How can you describe weather?

🖥 **Technology** Visit www.eduplace.com/scp/ to find out more about weather tools.

Focus On Literature

Read the page from the story. Then read the poem. Compare how the writers observe rain.

Rain
by Manya Stojic

A raindrop splashed.
"The rain is here!"
said the rhino.

"Porcupine smelled it.
The zebras saw it.
The baboons heard it.
And I felt it.
I must tell the lion."

D18 • Chapter 8

READING LINK

City Rain
by Rachel Field

Rain in the city!
   I love to see it fall
Slantwise where the buildings crowd
   Red brick and all,
Streets of shiny wetness
   Where the taxis go,
With people and umbrellas all
   Bobbing to and fro.

Sharing Ideas

1. **Write About It** How do the animals and the poet know it is raining?

2. **Talk About It** What is one thing in the story that real animals cannot do?

Lesson 3

What Are Clouds and Rain?

Science and You
If you see dark clouds in the sky, you know it might rain.

Inquiry Skill
Compare Look for ways that objects are alike and different.

What You Need

2 cups

water

tape

plastic wrap

grease pencil

Investigate

Water Changes

Steps

1. **Measure** Put the same amount of water into each cup. Cover one cup.

2. Mark the water level on each cup.

3. **Predict** Put the cups in a sunny place. Tell how the water might change.

4. **Observe** Look at the cups every day for a week. Record what you see.

STEP 1

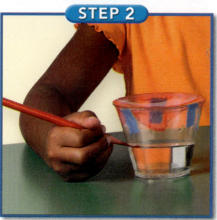
STEP 2

STEP 3

Think and Share

1. **Compare** How did the water change in each cup?

2. **Infer** Why do you think the water changed?

Investigate More!

Ask Questions What else can you do to make water change? Finish the question. What would happen to the water if I _____?

D21

Learn by Reading

Vocabulary

water cycle
cloud

Reading Skill
Cause and Effect

Water Cycle

Water moves from place to place. Sometimes it seems to disappear. Water moving from Earth to the sky and back again is called the **water cycle**.

▶ **CAUSE AND EFFECT**
What causes water to go into the air?

1 Heat from the Sun warms water. Some warm water goes into the air. You cannot see this water.

Kinds of Clouds

There are many kinds of clouds. They have different shapes and colors. Looking at clouds gives you clues about changing weather.

▶ **CAUSE AND EFFECT** What can clouds tell you about changing weather?

Cirrus clouds are thin and feathery. They mean it may rain in a day or two.

Cumulus clouds are puffy and white. They can turn gray and bring rain.

Stratus clouds are low and gray. They may bring rain or snow.

Lesson Wrap-Up

1. **Vocabulary** What is the **water cycle**?
2. **Reading Skill** What causes rain to fall?
3. **Compare** Draw two kinds of clouds. Tell how they are alike and different.

Technology Visit www.eduplace.com/scp/ to find out more about clouds.

Lesson 4

What Is Weather Like in Spring and Summer?

Science and You
Spring is a time when you may see flowers bloom.

Inquiry Skill
Communicate Tell other people what you know by drawing, speaking, or writing.

What You Need

2 cups

paper towels

seeds

water

Investigate

Grow Plants

Steps

1. Spray water on the paper towels. Fill each cup with paper towels.

2. Add seeds to each cup.

3. **Predict** Put the **winter** cup in a cold place. Put the **spring** cup in a warm place. Tell what you think will happen.

4. **Communicate** Look at the seeds after five days. Talk about how they have changed.

STEP 1

STEP 2

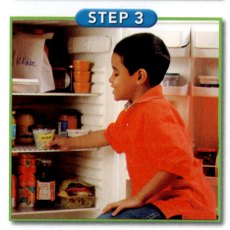
STEP 3

Think and Share

1. What helped the seeds grow?
2. **Infer** What happens to seeds in cold weather?

Investigate More!

Experiment Put the sprouted seeds in soil. Make a plan for caring for the plants. Follow your plan. Observe the plants for one month.

D27

Learn by Reading

Vocabulary
season
spring
summer

Reading Skill
Compare and Contrast

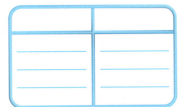

Spring

A **season** is a time of year that has its own kind of weather. **Spring** is the season that follows winter. There are more hours of daylight in spring than in winter.

In spring, the weather begins to get warmer. Warmer weather and spring rain help plants grow.

Spring plants begin to grow.

The warm weather and new plants make it easy for animals to find food. Animals that slept all winter are now awake. Birds that flew to other places in winter have come back. Many baby animals are born in spring.

goose with gosling

▶ **COMPARE AND CONTRAST**
How is spring different from winter?

Luna Moth in Spring

1. A caterpillar eats a leaf.
2. A caterpillar spins a cocoon.
3. A caterpillar changes to a moth.

Summer

Summer is the season that follows spring. Summer is the warmest season of the year. It has the most hours of daylight.

In summer, people try to find ways to stay cool. They wear clothing that keeps them cool. They might go swimming to cool off.

peach tree

How is this girl keeping cool?

Summer is the season for plants and animals to grow. Plants grow in the warm summer sun. Fruits form on trees and bushes. Young animals grow in summer, too. They learn to find their own food.

Growing plants are food for the lamb.

▶ **COMPARE AND CONTRAST**
How are spring and summer different?

Lesson Wrap-Up

1. **Vocabulary** What is a **season**?
2. **Reading Skill** How are spring and summer alike?
3. **Communicate** Write a story or draw a picture. Tell what happens to plants or animals in spring or summer.

 Technology Visit www.eduplace.com/scp/ to find out more about seasons.

Lesson 5

What Is Weather Like in Fall and Winter?

Science and You
When you know about the seasons, you know what kind of weather is coming next.

Inquiry Skill
Classify Group objects that are alike in some way.

What You Need

spinner

paper squares

crayons

paper

Investigate

What to Wear

Steps

1. Take turns spinning the spinner.

2. **Communicate** Name a clothing item you might wear in that season. Draw the item you name.

3. **Classify** Sort the clothing pictures by season. Label each group.

STEP 1

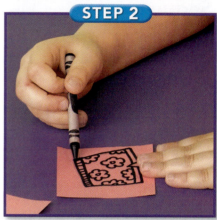
STEP 2

STEP 3

Think and Share

1. **Compare** How are all the summer clothes you drew alike?

2. What clothes keep you warm in cool weather?

Investigate More!

Solve a Problem Suppose your cousins are coming to visit you in winter. What kind of clothes would you tell them to bring?

D33

Learn by Reading

Vocabulary
fall
winter

Reading Skill
Sequence

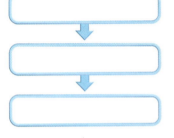

Fall

Fall is the season that follows summer. There are fewer hours of daylight in fall than in summer.

In fall, the weather gets cooler. People wear warmer clothes. Some leaves turn color and fall to the ground. Many fruits and vegetables are ripe.

Geese fly to warm places in fall.

In fall, animals get ready for cold weather. Some animals grow thicker fur to keep warm. Many animals store food for winter. Other animals move to places where there is more food. They will return in spring.

▶ **SEQUENCE** What season comes before winter?

A squirrel stores food for winter.

Winter

Winter is the season that follows fall. Winter has the fewest hours of daylight. It is the coldest season of the year. In some places, snow falls and water freezes. In other places, winter weather is warmer.

◀ winter where weather is warm ▶

◀ winter where weather is cold

▲ Why is it hard for animals to find food here?

Sometimes it is hard for animals to find food in winter. Some plants die. Many trees lose their leaves. Many animals eat food that they gathered in fall. Some animals sleep all winter.

▶ **SEQUENCE** What season follows winter?

The Pattern of Seasons

The seasons change in the same order every year. Living things change with the seasons.

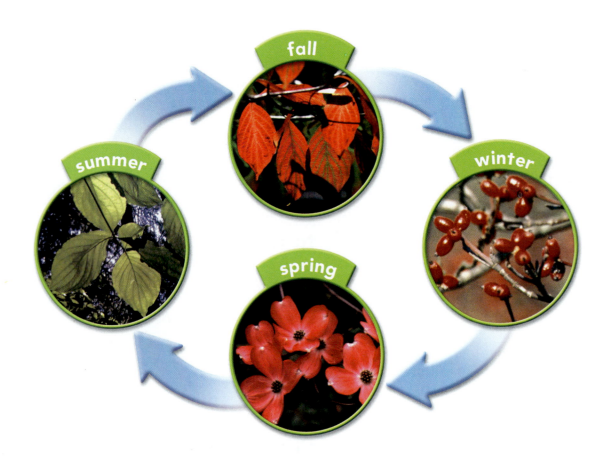

Lesson Wrap-Up

❶ **Vocabulary** What is **winter**?

❷ **Reading Skill** What season comes before fall?

❸ **Classify** Name three signs of fall.

🖥 **Technology** Visit www.eduplace.com/scp/ to find out more about seasons.

Math — Read a Bar Graph

Ms. Lane's class made a bar graph to show the weather for ten days.

1. How many days were sunny?
2. How many more days were cloudy than rainy?

Social Studies — Winter Weather

Winter is cold in many places. But winter is warm or hot in some places. Tell about winter where you live. Draw a picture of yourself in winter.

Winter is warm where I live.

D39

Chapter 8 Review and Test Prep

Visual Summary

Weather changes from day to day and from season to season.

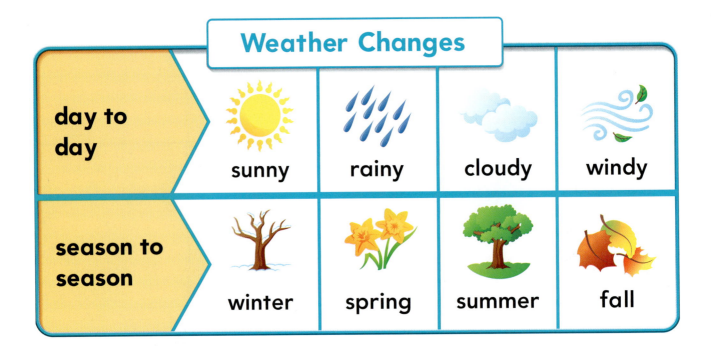

Main Ideas

1. What are some kinds of weather? (p. D8)
2. What can you tell by looking at clouds? (p. D24)
3. What is a season? (p. D28)
4. How does weather change from summer to fall? (p. D34)

SAT 10 Practice

Vocabulary and Science Skills

Choose the correct answer.

5. Which tool measures temperature?
   ○ ruler   ○ thermometer   ○ rain gauge

6. Many drops of water together form a _____.
   ○ cloud   ○ season   ○ temperature

7. Which is the coldest season of the year?
   ○ summer   ○ fall   ○ winter

8. Which is the warmest season of the year?
   ○ summer   ○ spring   ○ winter

9. Water moving from Earth to sky and back again is the _____.
   ○ spring   ○ water cycle   ○ weather

10. What always happens on windy days?
    ○ The ground is wet.   ○ The sky is sunny.
    ○ Tree branches move.

D41

Chapter 9
Changes in the Sky

Vocabulary Preview

Sun
star
planet
rotates
Moon
shadow

Sun
The Sun is the brightest space object in the day sky.

star
A star is a space object that makes its own light.

planet
A planet is a space object that moves around the Sun.

Moon
The Moon is a space object close to Earth.

Lesson 1

What Can You See in the Sky?

Science and You
You can tell whether it is day or night by looking at the sky.

Inquiry Skill
Observe Use your senses to find out about something.

What You Need

paper and pencil

drawing paper

crayons

Investigate

Observe the Sky

Steps

1. **Observe** Go outdoors and look at the sky. Make a list of what you see.
Safety: Do not look right at the Sun!

STEP 1

2. **Record Data** Go inside. Use your list. Draw a picture of what you saw.

STEP 2

3. **Compare** Ask others what they observed. Compare your drawings.

STEP 3

Think and Share

1. What did you and your classmates see in the day sky?
2. Did anything surprise you? Tell why.

Investigate More!

Work Together Observe the night sky. Draw what you see. Ask others what they saw. Tell how the night sky is different from the day sky.

D45

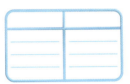

Vocabulary

Sun
star
planet

Reading Skill

Compare and Contrast

The Day Sky

The day sky is light. You may see clouds, birds, and the Sun. Airplanes and hot-air balloons may move across the sky. You might see a kite in the air.

an eagle in the day sky

The **Sun** is the brightest space object in the day sky. It warms the land, water, and air on Earth. The Sun makes the sky so bright that you cannot see other stars in the day.

▶ **MAIN IDEA** Name some objects you can see in the day sky.

Sun and clouds ▲

Sometimes you can see the Moon in the day sky. ▼

The Night Sky

The night sky is dark because there is no light from the Sun. You can see the Moon and stars at night. A **star** is a space object that makes its own light.

Sometimes you can see planets. A **planet** is a space object that moves around the Sun. Earth is a planet. Stars and planets look small because they are far away.

▶ **COMPARE AND CONTRAST** How are the day sky and the night sky different?

Lesson Wrap-Up

1. **Vocabulary** What makes the day sky bright?

2. **Reading Skill** Tell one way that the Sun and the Moon are alike. Tell one way that they are different.

3. **Observe** Tell what you see in the sky.

Technology Visit **www.eduplace.com/scp/** to find out more about day and night.

Lesson 2

What Causes Day and Night?

Science and You
Knowing how Earth moves helps you understand day and night.

Inquiry Skill
Infer Use what you observe and know to tell what you think.

What You Need

school picture

tape

flashlight

D50 • Chapter 9

Investigate

Day and Night

Steps

1. **Use Models** Tape your school picture on your clothes. The picture stands for your school on Earth.

STEP 1

2. **Infer** Have a partner shine a flashlight on the picture. The flashlight is the Sun. Tell whether it is day or night at school.

STEP 2

3. Turn until your school faces away from the Sun's light. Observe whether it is day or night.

STEP 3

Think and Share

1. When was it day at school? When was it night?
2. **Predict** What will happen if you keep turning? Try it.

Investigate More!

Experiment Mark on a globe where you live. Then use a flashlight and turn the globe to model day and night where you live.

D51

Learn by Reading

Vocabulary
rotates

Reading Skill
Cause and Effect

Day on Earth

Earth **rotates**, or spins. As Earth rotates, the Sun shines on different parts of it. It is day when the part of Earth where you live faces the Sun. The sky is light.

▶ **CAUSE AND EFFECT** Why is the sky light during the day?

It is easier to see outside during the day.

Night on Earth

It is night when the part of Earth where you live faces away from the Sun. The sky is dark.

It takes 24 hours for Earth to rotate one time. Earth keeps rotating. Day and night repeat.

 **CAUSE AND EFFECT** Why is the sky dark at night?

You need lights to see at night.

Lesson Wrap-Up

1. **Vocabulary** How does Earth move when it **rotates**?

2. **Reading Skill** What causes day on Earth?

3. **Infer** If it is night where you are, where do you think it is day?

Technology Visit www.eduplace.com/scp/ to find out more about Earth's rotation.

Lesson 3

How Does the Moon Seem to Change?

Science and You
Knowing how the Moon changes can help you understand the night sky.

Inquiry Skill
Use Models Use a model to find how the Moon seems to change.

What You Need

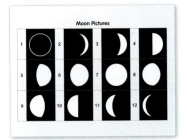

Moon pictures

scissors

stapler

D56 • Chapter 9

Investigate

Moon Changes

Steps

1. Cut out Moon pictures.
   Safety: Scissors are sharp!

STEP 1

2. **Use Numbers** Pile the pictures in order from 1 to 12. Staple the pictures together to make a book.

STEP 2

3. **Use Models** Hold one side of the book in one hand. Flip the pages with your other hand.

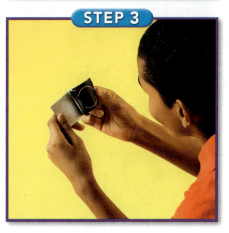
STEP 3

Think and Share

1. What did you observe about the Moon when you flipped the pages?
2. What do you think your model shows about the real Moon?

Investigate More!

Experiment How can you predict what the Moon will look like on a cloudy night? Make a plan to find out. Tell how your plan works.

Learn by Reading

▶ **Vocabulary**
Moon

▶ **Reading Skill**
Sequence

The Moon

The **Moon** is a space object close to Earth. From Earth you can see dark spots on the Moon. Some spots are pits called craters.

Astronauts have visited the Moon.

D58 • Chapter 9 • Lesson 3

The Sun is a star that makes its own light. The Moon is not a star. It does not make its own light. We see the part of the Moon that the Sun is shining on.

▶ **CAUSE AND EFFECT** Why does the Moon seem bright?

Light from the Sun lets us see the Moon.

Sun

Earth

Moon

new Moon

first quarter Moon

The Changing Moon

The Moon's shape looks different every night. The Moon is round, but we may not see all of it.

The Moon moves around Earth. We see different parts of the Moon's lighted side as it moves. It takes about 28 days for the Moon to move around Earth. Then it looks the same again.

▶ **SEQUENCE** If there is a full Moon tonight, what will the Moon look like after 28 days?

full Moon

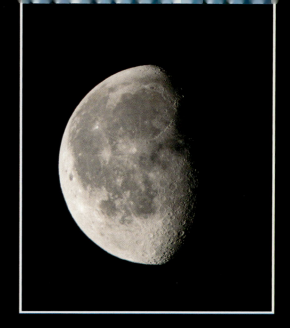
last quarter Moon

Lesson Wrap-Up

1. **Vocabulary** How is the **Moon** different from the Sun?

2. **Reading Skill** How does the Moon seem to change?

3. **Use Models** How can a model show how the Moon changes?

Technology Visit www.eduplace.com/scp/ to find out more about the Moon.

Biography

Galileo Galilei
Scientist

Galileo Galilei was a scientist. He lived in Italy 400 years ago. He heard about a new tool called a telescope. Galileo made one for himself. It was a long tube made of wood. It had lenses on each end.

SOCIAL STUDIES LINK

The telescope made objects look bigger and brighter. Galileo saw craters on the Moon when he looked through his telescope. He was the first person to see moons orbiting the planet Jupiter.

Sharing Ideas

1. **Write About It** Why is a telescope helpful to a scientist?
2. **Talk About It** How did Galileo help others understand the sky?

Lesson 4

How Does the Sun Seem to Move?

Science and You
You can check your shadow to guess the time of day.

Inquiry Skill
Predict Use what you know to tell what you think might happen.

What You Need

crayons

Sun chart

clock

D64 • Chapter 9

Investigate

Sun Changes

Steps

1. **Observe** Go outdoors in the morning. Find where the Sun is in the sky.
Safety: Do not look right at the Sun!

STEP 1

2. **Record Data** Use a chart to show where the Sun is. Go out at noon. Record what you find.

STEP 2

3. **Predict** Look at your data. Predict where the Sun will be next. Check your prediction.

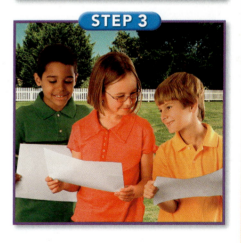
STEP 3

Think and Share

1. What did you observe about the Sun?
2. How did your prediction compare to what happened?

Investigate More!

Experiment Make a plan to observe how the Sun changes shadows during the day. Talk with the class about what you learn.

Learn by Reading

Vocabulary
shadow

Reading Skill
Draw Conclusions

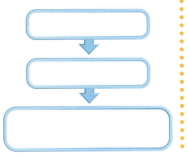

The Sun

The Sun seems to move from one side of the sky to the other. The Sun is low in the sky in the morning. It is higher in the sky at noon. The Sun is low in the sky late in the day.

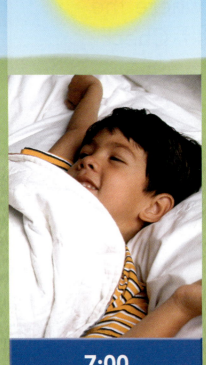

7:00

9:00

The Sun is not moving. Earth is moving. As Earth rotates, we see the Sun, Moon, or stars in different parts of the sky.

▶ **DRAW CONCLUSIONS** Where is the Sun when you eat breakfast?

12:00   3:00   5:00

The Sun and Shadows

A **shadow** forms when an object blocks light. Shadows change during the day because the Sun is in different parts of the sky.

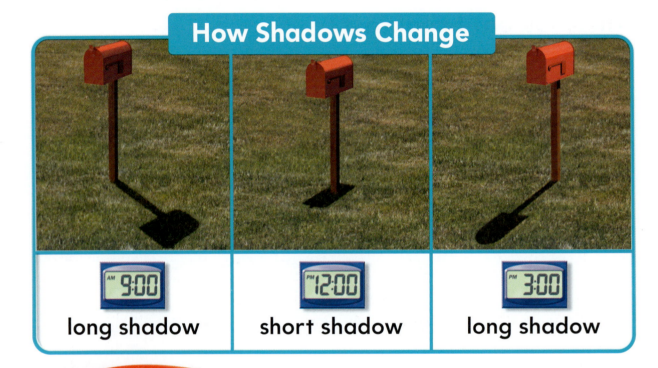

How Shadows Change

long shadow	short shadow	long shadow
AM 9:00	PM 12:00	PM 3:00

Lesson Wrap-Up

1. **Vocabulary** How does a **shadow** form?
2. **Reading Skill** What happens to the Sun in the sky as Earth rotates?
3. **Predict** Will the shadow of a tree be long or short at 4 o'clock?

Technology Visit www.eduplace.com/scp/ to find out more about the Sun.

LINKS for Home and School

Math   Measure Shadows

Work with a partner. Measure each others' shadows many times during the day. Measure from your foot to the end of the shadow. Record what you observe. Tell how your shadow changed.

My Shadow

Time of Day	Where the Sun Is	Length of Shadow
_____ o'clock	high in the sky / low in the sky	_____ feet
_____ o'clock	high in the sky / low in the sky	_____ feet
_____ o'clock	high in the sky / low in the sky	_____ feet

Language Arts   Write a Story

Think about what you see in the day sky or the night sky. Write a story about what you see.

Chapter 9 Review and Test Prep

Visual Summary

Day and night happen when Earth rotates.

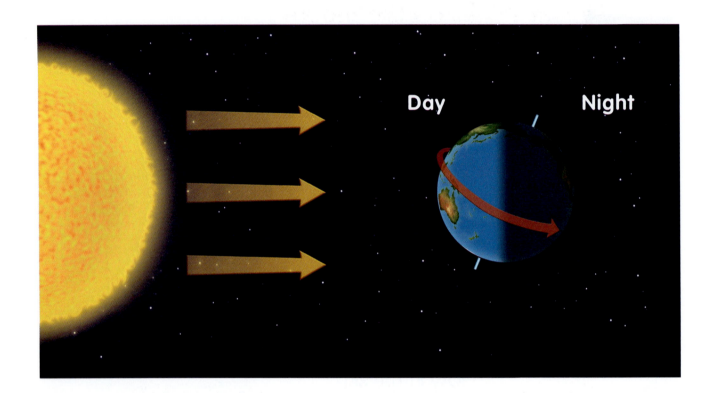

Main Ideas

1. What can you see in the day sky? (pp. D46–D47)

2. What can you see in the night sky? (p. D48)

3. What causes day and night? (pp. D52–D55)

4. Draw pictures to show four different ways the Moon can look. (pp. D60–D61)

SAT 10 Practice

Vocabulary and Science Skills

Choose the correct answer.

5. Which shines on the moon?
   ○ Earth   ○ the planets   ○ the Sun

6. Shadows form when objects block ____.
   ○ time   ○ light   ○ planets

7. A round, bright moon is a ____.
   ○ new Moon   ○ full Moon
   ○ last quarter Moon

8. Which warms land and water on Earth?
   ○ shadows   ○ the Sun   ○ the Moon

9. What causes day and night?
   ○ Earth rotates.   ○ The Sun moves.
   ○ The Moon changes.

10. Why do you not see stars in the day?
    ○ Stars are gone.   ○ The Sun is bright.
    ○ The Moon is round.

Wrap-Up

Discover!

Where are the stars during the day?

Stars are always in the sky. During the day, the Sun makes the sky too bright to see other stars. At night, the Sun does not shine on your part of Earth. Then you can see the light from other stars.

Go to **www.eduplace.com/scp/** to find the stars during the day.

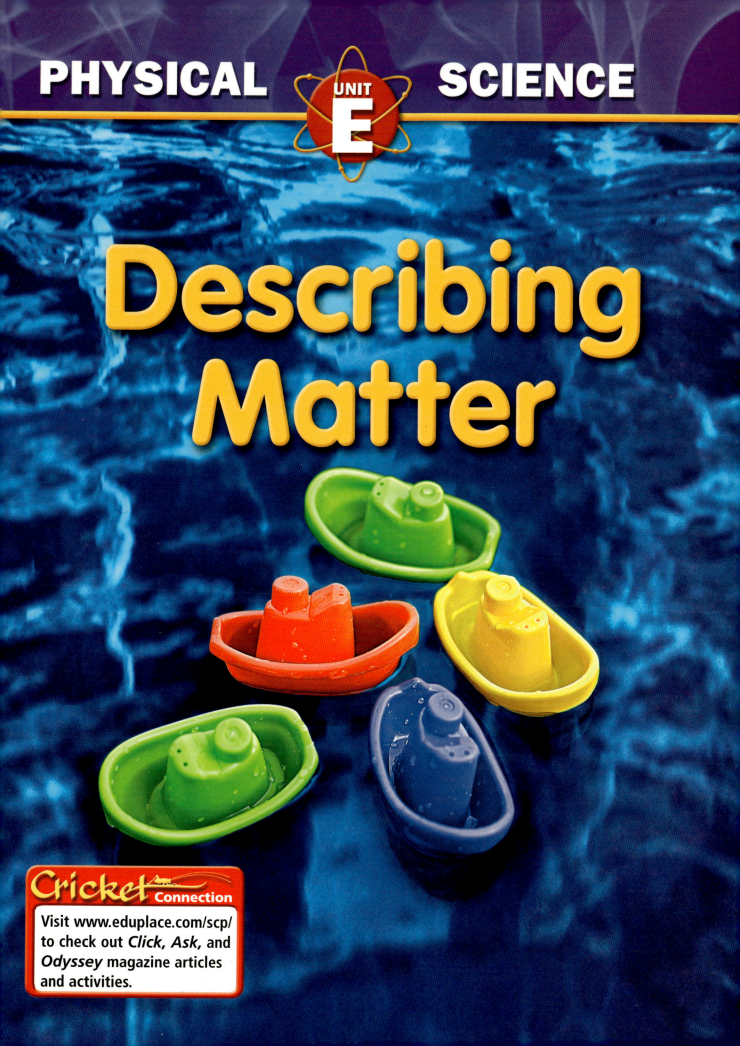

PHYSICAL SCIENCE
UNIT E

Describing Matter

Reading in Science E2

Chapter 10
Observing Objects E4

Chapter 11
Changes in Matter E34

Independent Reading

| Sink or Float | Louis Braille | Balloons |

Discover!

Will a pumpkin float in water?

Think about this question as you read. You will have the answer by the end of the unit.

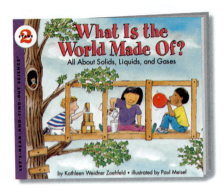

What Is the World Made Of?

by Kathleen Weidner Zoehfeld
illustrated by Paul Meisel

Walls and blocks, dolls and socks. Milk and lemonade. Rocks and trees. All of these things are made of matter.

The air in the breeze that blows the leaves. Water flowing in the creek. Everything on earth is made of matter.

Chapter 10
Observing Objects

Vocabulary Preview

matter
property
magnify
weigh
magnet
attracts
repel
sink
float

matter

Matter is what all things are made of.

magnify

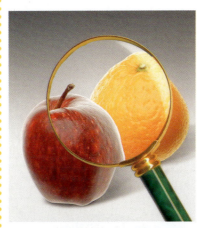

To magnify is to make something look larger.

magnet

A magnet is an object that pulls iron and steel toward it.

sink

To sink is to drop to the bottom of water.

Lesson 1

How Can You Describe Matter?

Science and You
Your senses tell you about objects around you.

Inquiry Skill
Classify You can use your senses to group objects that are alike.

What You Need

objects

index cards

marker

Investigate

Classify Objects

Steps

1. **Classify** Decide how the objects are alike. Sort them into groups.

2. **Record Data** Name your groups. Write the name of each group on a different card.

3. **Communicate** Tell how the objects in each group are alike. Write your ideas on the cards.

STEP 1

STEP 2

STEP 3

Think and Share

1. How did you sort the objects?

2. Why might one person's ideas about sorting be different from another person's?

Investigate More!

Work Together Work with a partner. Talk about other ways to sort the objects. How many groups can you make?

E7

Learn by Reading

Vocabulary
matter
property

Reading Skill
Main Idea and Details

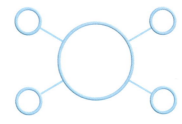

Matter and Your Senses

Matter is what all things are made of. People use their senses to learn about matter. Sight, smell, hearing, touch, and taste are senses. You see and smell a flower. Many flowers have pleasant smells. You feel a kitten's fur. It is soft.

You can see, smell, touch, and taste your lunch.

You can use your senses to compare these dogs.

Comparing Dogs

Sense	Dog A	Dog B
Hearing	low sound	high sound
Sight	large and brown	small and white
Touch	smooth	rough

▶ **MAIN IDEA** What can your senses tell you about different things?

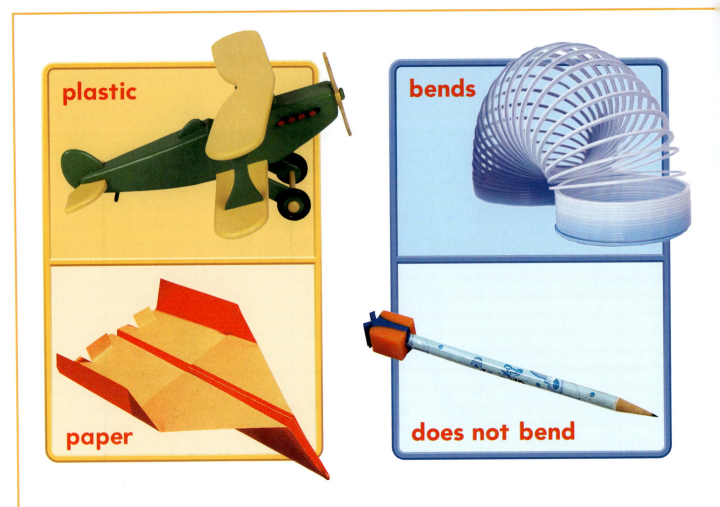

Observing Properties

You can use your senses to describe a property of an object. A **property** is anything that you learn about an object by using your senses. You can see an object's size, shape, and color. You can see what it is made of. You can tell how it sounds, smells, and tastes.

● **MAIN IDEA** How can you tell about the properties of an object?

Lesson Wrap-Up

❶ **Vocabulary** What is a **property**?

❷ **Reading Skill** How can your senses help you compare objects?

❸ **Classify** How could you group these objects?

Technology Visit www.eduplace.com/scp/ to find out more about matter.

Lesson 2

How Can You Use Tools to Observe?

Science and You
Using tools can help you compare objects.

Inquiry Skill
Measure Use a tool to find out how much or how many.

What You Need

objects

balance

hand lens

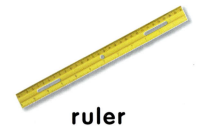
ruler

Investigate

Use Tools

Steps

1. **Measure** Use a ruler to measure an object. Tell what you find.

2. **Compare** Use a balance to compare the weights of two objects. Tell what you find.

3. **Observe** Use a hand lens to look closely at one of the objects. Tell what you see.

Think and Share

1. What did you learn about each object?
2. How did the tools help you?

Investigate More!

Solve a Problem Everyone in art class wants clay. How can you use a tool to make sure each child gets the same amount?

E13

Learn by Reading

Vocabulary
magnify
weigh

Reading Skill
Main Idea and Details

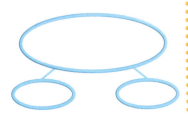

A Tool to Magnify

Scientists use tools to learn about the properties of matter. You can use tools, too.

A hand lens can magnify an object. To **magnify** is to make something look larger.

How can a hand lens help this girl learn about the properties of a ladybug?

without a hand lens

with a hand lens

Objects look different when you look at them with a hand lens. You can see tiny parts that you cannot see without a hands lens.

▶ **MAIN IDEA** How can a hand lens help you observe an object?

A Tool to Weigh

You **weigh** an object to find how heavy it is. How much an object weighs is one of its properties. A balance tells whether one object weighs more than another.

The balance is lower on the side with the blue toy because the blue toy weighs more than the orange toy.

Tools for Length

You can use rulers or measuring tapes to find how long or tall objects are. You also can measure with things such as paper clips or your fingers.

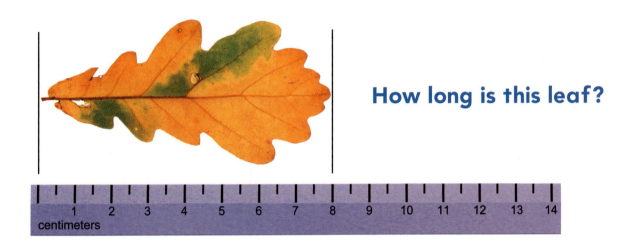

How long is this leaf?

▶ **MAIN IDEA** What tool tells you which object weighs more than another?

Lesson Wrap-Up

1. **Vocabulary** What does <mark>magnify</mark> mean?
2. **Reading Skill** What tools can you use to learn about the properties of matter?
3. **Measure** Which tool measures length?

🖥 **Technology** visit www.eduplace.com/scp/ to find out more about tools.

E17

Lesson 3

What Does a Magnet Attract?

Science and You
People use magnets to pick up objects and to hold things.

Inquiry Skill
Infer Use what you observe and know to tell what you think.

What You Need

magnet

objects

magnet chart

Investigate

Use Magnets

Steps

1. **Observe** Test each object with a magnet.

2. **Record Data** Decide whether the magnet pulls the object. Record your results.

Object	Magnet Pulls	Magnet Does Not Pull
paper		✓

3. **Compare** Tell how the objects that were pulled and not pulled to the magnet are different.

Think and Share

1. **Infer** What is the same about the objects that the magnet pulled?

2. **Predict** Think of an object that you did not test. Do you think the magnet will pull it? Why or why not?

Investigate More!

Experiment Will a magnet attract an object if there is something between the magnet and the object? Make a plan for finding an answer.

E19

Learn by Reading

Vocabulary
magnet
attracts
repel

Reading Skill
Cause and Effect

Magnets

A **magnet** is an object that pulls iron and steel toward it. A magnet **attracts** objects when it pulls them. Sometimes a magnet attracts things without touching them. A magnet does not attract everything. It will not attract paper, wood, or plastic objects.

Which materials does the magnet attract?

If a magnet attracts an object, you can say that is a property of the object. It is another way to describe the object.

▶ **MAIN IDEA** What does a magnet attract?

objects the magnet attracts

objects the magnet does not attract

E21

These magnets have different poles next to each other.

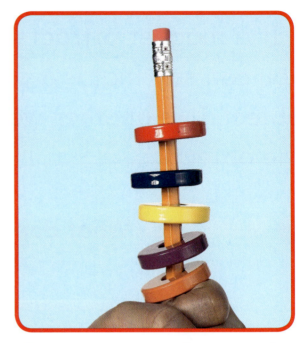

These magnets have poles that are alike next to each other.

Magnets Act on Each Other

A magnet has different parts. Parts called poles have the strongest pull. Every magnet has two poles. When you put two magnets together, you can feel the poles act on each other.

Poles that are different attract each other. Poles that are alike push away, or **repel**, each other.

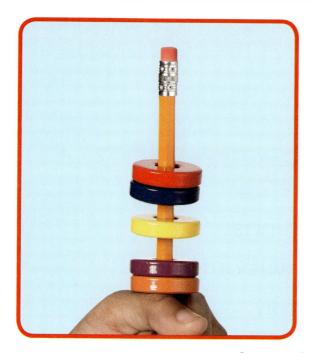 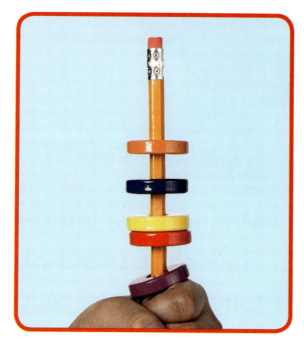

Are the poles next to each other alike or different?

CAUSE AND EFFECT What causes magnets to repel each other?

Lesson Wrap-Up

1. **Vocabulary** How do magnets act when they **repel** each other?

2. **Reading Skill** Why are some objects attracted by a magnet?

3. **Infer** Part of one magnet pulls part of another magnet. What can you infer about the two parts of the magnets?

Technology Visit www.eduplace.com/scp to find out more about magnets.

Focus On Technology

Mighty Magnets

Magnets are interesting things. They can attract objects without touching them. Magnets can even attract objects if there is something between the magnet and the object.

The sled has metal on it. The magnet can move the sled without touching it.

READING LINK

The fish has steel on its mouth. The magnet on the fishing pole attracts the fish through water. ▶

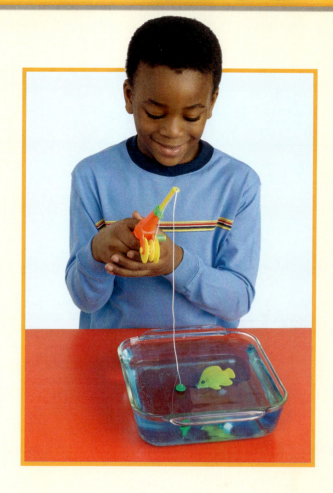

◀ There are tiny pieces of iron in the bag. When the magnet moves, the iron makes different patterns.

Sharing Ideas

1. **Write About It** Use your own words to write about ways that magnets attract objects.

2. **Talk About It** What are some other ways that magnets could be used?

Lesson 4

What Floats and What Sinks?

Science and You
When you go swimming, it is good to know what things float.

Inquiry Skill
Predict Use what you know to tell what will happen.

What You Need

tub

water

objects

float-and-sink chart

Investigate

Float or Sink

Steps

1. Pour water into a tub.

2. **Predict** Choose an object. Decide if it will float or sink. Write your prediction.

3. **Observe** Put the object in the water. Watch what happens.

4. **Record Data** Write what happened. Test other objects.

//STEP 1

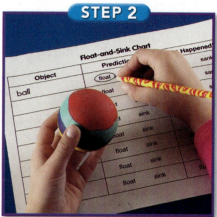//STEP 2

//STEP 3

Think and Share

1. Compare your prediction with what you observed.

2. **Infer** What is the same about the objects that floated?

Investigate More!

Experiment Take a ball of clay. Change its shape to make it float. Draw the shape you made.

E27

Learn by Reading

Vocabulary

sink
float

Reading Skill

Categorize and Classify

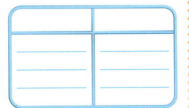

Floating and Sinking

Some objects **sink**, or drop to the bottom of water. Other objects **float**, or stay on top of water. Floating and sinking are properties of an object. You can group objects that float. You can also group objects that sink.

Which objects float?
Which objects sink?

E28 • Chapter 10 • Lesson 4

Sometimes the weight of an object helps it float. Light objects often float. Sometimes the shape of an object helps it float. Flat objects often float. Sometimes objects float because they have air in them.

▶ **CLASSIFY** What are some objects that float?

Making Objects Sink

You can cause some floating objects to sink. Sometimes you can make an object sink by changing its shape or filling it with water.

The cup sinks when it fills with water.

Lesson Wrap-Up

❶ **Vocabulary** What does **float** mean?

❷ **Reading Skill** Name two things that sink.

❸ **Predict** Look at these objects. Which one is likely to float? Tell why.

🔌 **Technology** Visit www.eduplace.com/scp/ to find out more about floating and sinking.

Math Read a Bar Graph

Bob dipped different magnets into a pile of paper clips. The graph shows the number of paper clips each magnet attracted.

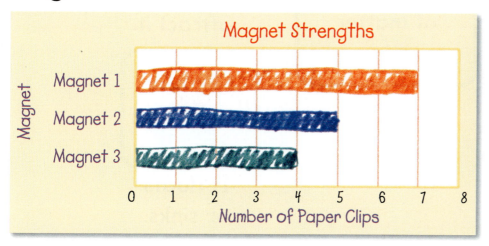

1. How many paper clips did each magnet attract?

2. What is the difference in the number of paper clips for magnets 1 and 3?

Language Arts Write a Letter

Write a letter to a friend about your favorite food. Tell how the food looks, tastes, feels, sounds, and smells.

Chapter 10 Review and Test Prep

Visual Summary

Matter has many properties.

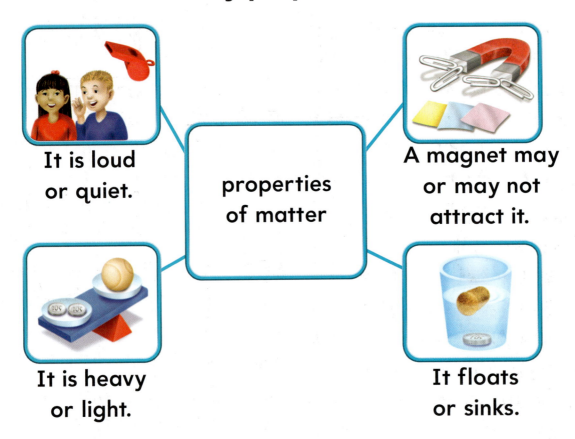

It is loud or quiet.

properties of matter

A magnet may or may not attract it.

It is heavy or light.

It floats or sinks.

Main Ideas

1. What are an object's properties? (p. E10)

2. What does a balance tell you? (p. E16)

3. Two objects push away from each other. Use another word to tell how the magnets act. (p. E22)

4. Why do some things sink? (p. E29)

SAT 10 Practice

Vocabulary and Science Skills

Choose the correct answer.

5. All things are made of ____.
○ senses   ○ matter   ○ property

6. Which can magnify an object?
○ hand lens   ○ ruler   ○ balance

7. Which attracts iron and steel?
○ ruler   ○ wood   ○ magnet

8. Sight is one of your ____.
○ objects   ○ senses   ○ tools

9. Which is likely to sink?
○ toy boat   ○ marble   ○ leaf

10. Different poles on magnets ____ each other.
○ repel   ○ attract   ○ float

Chapter 11
Changes in Matter

E34 • Chapter 11

Vocabulary Preview

- solid
- liquid
- gas
- freeze
- melt
- evaporate
- mixture
- dissolve

solid
A solid is matter that has its own shape.

liquid
A liquid is matter that flows and takes the shape of its container.

gas
A gas is matter that changes shape to fill all the space it is in.

melt
To melt is to change from a solid to a liquid.

Lesson 1

What Are Solids, Liquids, and Gases?

Science and You
Water can spill because it is a liquid.

Inquiry Skill
Compare Look carefully to see how objects are alike or different.

What You Need

containers

colored water

rock

balloon

Investigate

Compare Matter

Steps

1. **Observe** Gently squeeze a balloon. Tell what happens to the shape.

2. **Compare** Squeeze a rock. Put it in each container. Tell what happens to the shape of the rock.

3. **Communicate** Pour water into each container. Tell what happens to the shape of the water.

STEP 1

STEP 2

STEP 3

Think and Share

1. What happened when you squeezed the balloon?

2. Compare the rock and the water in the containers. How were they different?

Investigate More!

Solve a Problem Suppose you want to send one of the objects to someone who lives far away. Which object would be easiest to pack? Why?

Learn by Reading

Vocabulary
- solid
- liquid
- gas

Reading Skill
Categorize and Classify

Solids

Matter is what all things are made of. Three forms of matter are solids, liquids, and gases. A **solid** is matter that has its own shape. Rocks and soil are solids. Objects in your room are solids, too.

A solid keeps its shape unless you do something to change it. You can cut, tear, bend, or break a solid to change its shape.

▶ **CLASSIFY** What are three things that are solids?

What solids do you see in this picture?

Liquids

You can pour water. You can pour milk and juice. Water, milk, and juice are liquids. A **liquid** is matter that flows and takes the shape of its container. A liquid does not have its own shape. It does not always fill its container.

▼ How can you change the shape of a liquid?

E40 • Chapter 11 • Lesson 1

Gases

The air around you is a gas. A <u>**gas**</u> <u>is matter that changes shape to fill</u> <u>all the space it is in.</u>

▼ A gas spreads out to fill a balloon.

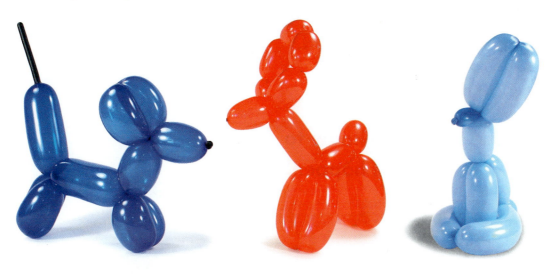

▶ **CLASSIFY** What forms of matter do not have their own shape?

Lesson Wrap-Up

1. **Vocabulary** What is a **liquid**?
2. **Reading Skill** What form of matter are milk, juice, and water?
3. **Compare** How are solids, liquids, and gases different?

Technology Visit www.eduplace.com/scp/ to find out more about matter.

E41

Lesson 2

What Do Heating and Cooling Do?

Science and You
Snow melts when it is heated.

Inquiry Skill
Predict Use what you know to tell what you think will happen.

What You Need

bags of ice

warm and cold water

timer

Investigate

Predict Changes

Steps

1. Put one bag of ice in a bowl of cold water. Put the other bag of ice in a bowl of warm water.

2. **Predict** Record what you think will happen to the ice in each bowl.

3. **Observe** Wait five minutes. Look to see how the ice cubes changed.

Think and Share

1. **Communicate** Tell others how the ice changed.

2. **Infer** Why did the bags of ice change in different ways?

Investigate More!

Experiment How can you make the water change back into a solid? Think of a plan for finding an answer. Then test your plan.

Learn by Reading

Vocabulary

freeze
melt
evaporate

Reading Skill
Cause and Effect

Water Changes

Water on Earth can change from one form to another. Water freezes when it gets very cold. To **freeze** is to change from a liquid to a solid. Ice is solid water. You freeze water to make ice cubes.

Some solids melt when they are heated. To **melt** is to change from a solid to a liquid. When ice gets warm, it melts. A frozen pond melts in spring.

Juice changes from a liquid to a solid when it freezes. It changes from a solid back to a liquid when it melts.

A Pond Changes

Fall
The water in the pond is liquid.

Winter
The water on the top of the pond is solid.

Spring
The water in the pond is liquid again.

▶ **CAUSE AND EFFECT** What causes the pond to change from season to season?

Liquid to Gas

Water on Earth can be a gas, too. Water evaporates when it is heated. To **evaporate** is to change from a liquid to a gas. You cannot see water when it is a gas.

Heat from the Sun made the puddles evaporate.

▶ **CAUSE AND EFFECT** What causes water to change into a gas?

Lesson Wrap-Up

1. **Vocabulary** What happens when water **evaporates**?

2. **Reading Skill** What causes liquid water to change into ice?

3. **Predict** Look at this picture. What will happen to the liquid water? Why?

Technology Visit www.eduplace.com/scp/ to find out more about water changing form.

Focus On Literature

READING LINK

Read this poem to find what icicles are made of.

Ice Cycle
by Mary Ann Hoberman

I've always thought it rather nice
That water freezes into ice.
I'm also pleased that it is true
That ice melts back to water, too.
But even so I find it strange
The way that ice and water change
And how a single water drop
Can fathom when it's time to stop
Its downward drip and go ahead
And start an icicle instead.

Sharing Ideas

1. **Write About It** What are icicles made of?
2. **Talk About It** What is the temperature like when an icicle forms?

Lesson 3

What Happens When You Mix Things?

Science and You
You make a mixture when you put fruit and milk on cereal.

Inquiry Skill
Observe Use your senses to help you understand something that happens.

What You Need

bowl

spoon

warm water

salt

Investigate

Make a Mixture

Steps

1. **Predict** Put salt in a bowl. Add water to the bowl. Tell what you think will happen when you stir the mixture.

2. Stir. Tell how the mixture looks. **Safety:** Do not taste the mixture!

3. **Observe** Put the mixture in a warm place. Look at what happens after a few days.

Think and Share

1. How does your prediction compare to what happens?
2. **Communicate** Tell what you learned about the mixture.

Investigate More!

Work Together Try mixing other things with water. You might use solids or other liquids. Share what you observe.

E49

Learn by Reading

Vocabulary

mixture
dissolve

Reading Skill

Main Idea and Details

Solid Mixtures

A **mixture** is two or more kinds of matter put together. Some mixtures are all solids. You have a mixture when you make a sandwich.

What are the solids that make up this mixture?

Mixtures can be taken apart. You can take parts off your sandwich. You can use a magnet to pull iron or steel from some mixtures. You can even use a screen to sift out the small parts of a mixture.

▶ **MAIN IDEA** How can you make a mixture?

Mixing Solids and Liquids

You can make a mixture with solids and liquids. Some solids **dissolve**, or mix completely, in water. Sugar dissolves in water. You cannot see it, but it is there.

◀ A drink mix dissolves in water.

Lesson Wrap-Up

1. **Vocabulary** What is a **mixture**?

2. **Reading Skill** Are toys in a toy box a mixture? Tell why or why not.

3. **Observe** What are different ways a mixture can look?

Technology Visit www.eduplace.com/scp/ to find out more about mixtures.

LINKS for Home and School

Math — Write Number Sentences

Mix 10 buttons and 10 marbles. Take out a handful of the mixture.

$$4+2=6$$
$$4-2=2$$

1. How many buttons and marbles did you take out?

2. Which kind of object do you have more of? How many more?

Art — Sand Paintings

Native Americans tell stories with sand paintings. They mix many colors of sand. Use sand, rocks, or other solids to make a picture that tells a story.

Chapter 11 Review and Test Prep

Visual Summary

Matter has different forms.

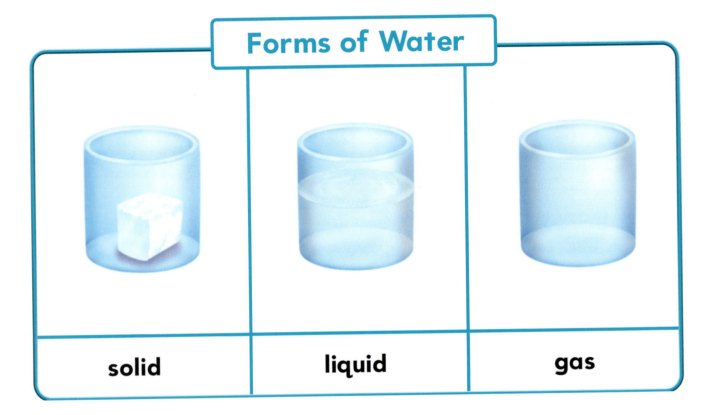

Main Ideas

1. How can you tell if an object is a solid? (p. E38)

2. How are gases and liquids alike? (pp. E40–E41)

3. What are three ways that water can change? (pp. E44–E46)

4. Why is a sandwich a mixture? (pp. E50–E51)

SAT 10 Practice

Vocabulary and Science Skills

Choose the correct answer.

5. Which substance is a gas?
   ○ air   ○ cookies   ○ milk

6. When water changes to a solid, it ____.
   ○ freezes   ○ melts   ○ evaporates

7. Which has its own shape?
   ○ solid   ○ liquid   ○ gas

8. When a liquid changes to a gas, it ____.
   ○ freezes   ○ melts   ○ evaporates

9. Which is a mixture?
   ○ water   ○ sugar   ○ sandwich

10. Which can dissolve in water?
    ○ sugar   ○ cheese   ○ bread

Wrap-Up

Discover!

Will a pumpkin float in water?

A pumpkin has a large center space filled with air and seeds. The air helps the pumpkin float. If you fill that center space with water, the pumpkin will sink a little lower.

Go to **www.eduplace.com/scp/** to test which objects sink and which objects float.

PHYSICAL SCIENCE
UNIT F

Energy Sources and Motion

Reading in Science F2

Chapter 12
Heat, Light, and Sound F4

Chapter 13
Moving Faster and Slower F32

Independent Reading

- It's Too Loud 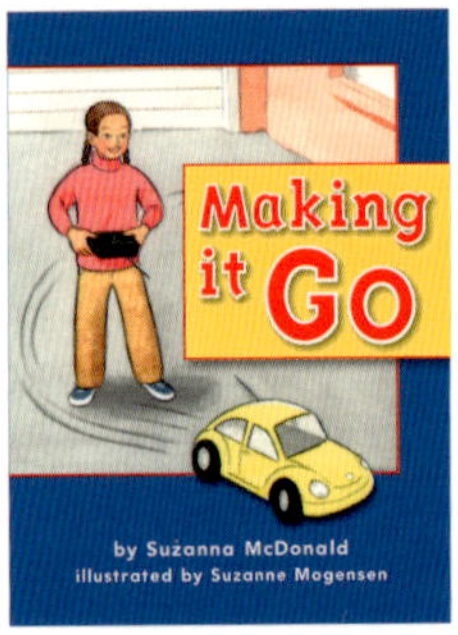
- Making It Go 
- Night Lights

Energy
Heat, Light, and Fuel

by Darlene Stille
illustrated by Sheree Boyd

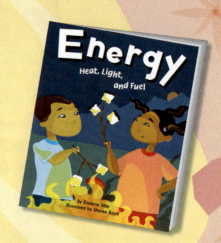

It's morning. You stretch your arms out wide. You jump out of bed. You are full of energy. You use that energy to get things done!

Energy gets lots of things done. There are many forms of energy. Energy heats your house. It lights up lamps. It makes cars, trucks, and buses go.

Reading in Science
Strategy: Question

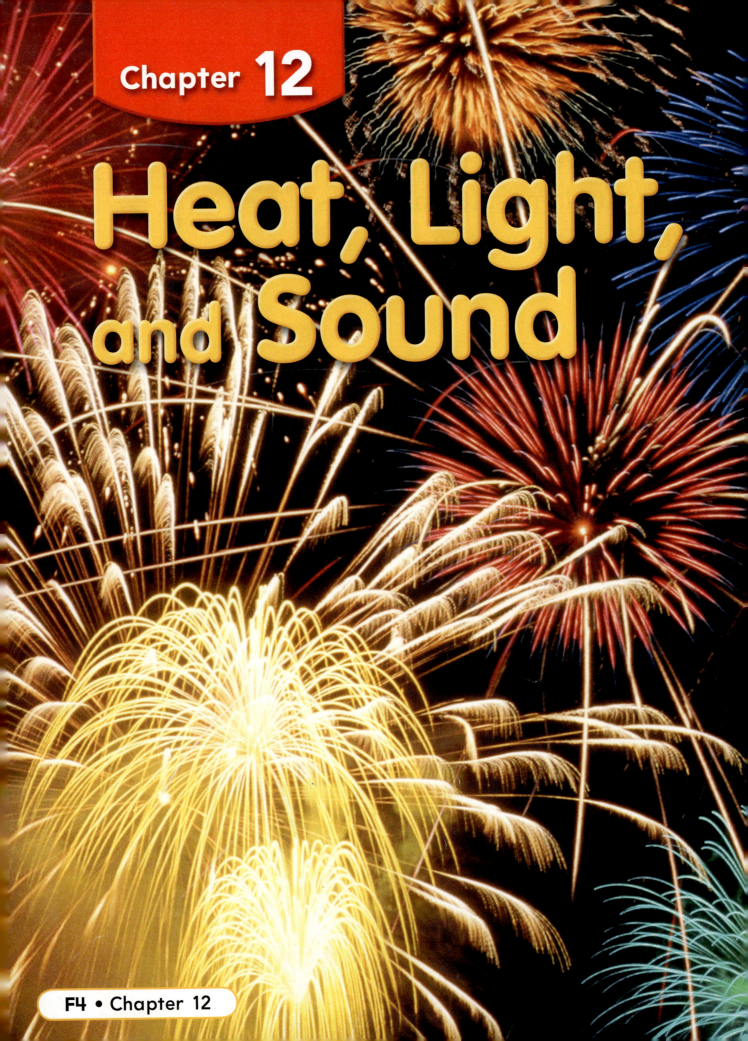

Chapter 12

Heat, Light, and Sound

Vocabulary Preview

energy
heat
light
shadow
sound
vibrates
pitch
volume

heat
Heat is a kind of energy that makes things warm.

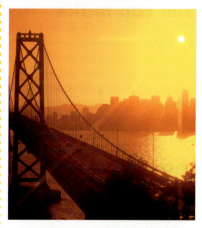

light
Light is a kind of energy that you can see.

sound
Sound is a kind of energy that you can hear.

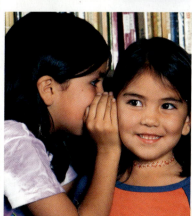

volume
Volume is how loud or soft a sound is.

Lesson 1

Where Does Heat Come From?

Science and You
Heat from the Sun can make you hot and thirsty.

Inquiry Skill
Measure You can use a tool to find out how much or how many.

What You Need

3 jars

water and sand

3 thermometers

heat chart

Investigate

Measure Heat

Steps

1. Fill one jar with water. Fill another jar with sand. Leave one jar empty.

2. **Measure** Put a thermometer in each jar. Read each thermometer. Record each temperature.

3. **Record Data** Put the jars in a sunny place. Record the temperatures every 30 minutes.

STEP 1

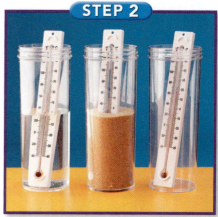
STEP 2

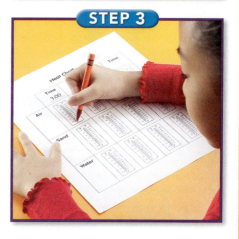
STEP 3

Think and Share

1. **Compare** Which jar had the warmest temperature after 90 minutes?

2. **Infer** Why was one jar warmer?

Investigate More!

Experiment Try the same experiment another day. Is your data the same as it was the first time? Why do you think that happened?

Learn by Reading

Vocabulary

energy
heat

Reading Skill

Cause and Effect

Heat

Energy is something that can cause change or do work. Heat is a kind of energy that makes things warm. Earth gets heat from the Sun.

The Sun warms Earth's air, water, and land. The Sun also warms you. You feel warm when you stand in the Sun. You feel cooler when you move to a shady place.

Heat comes from other places, too. Fire gives off heat. So do a lit stove, a burning candle, and a turned-on light bulb. Rubbing things together can make them give off heat, too.

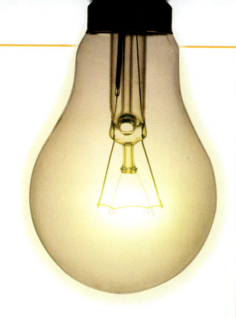

▲ Be careful! Light bulbs get very hot.

🟠 **CAUSE AND EFFECT** What warms Earth's air, land, and water?

◀ Heat warms your home.

What happens when you rub your hands together? Try it! ▶

F9

Heat Changes Things

Heat can make things change. Heat from your body makes your sheets warm. Heat from the Sun can make a metal slide too hot to use. Heat from a flame melts a candle. Heat makes butter soft.

▲ Heat makes ice melt.

▼ Heat cooks food.

A fire gives off heat when it burns. You feel the heat as the fire warms your body. Heat spreads out and warms things around it.

Heat can move things. Look at the picture. Heat from the flames moves the air. The air moves the windmill.

Heat can make things move. ▼

▶ **CAUSE AND EFFECT** What are some ways that heat causes change?

Lesson Wrap-Up

❶ **Vocabulary** What is **energy**?

❷ **Reading Skill** How can heat from the Sun or a fire make your body feel different?

❸ **Measure** How could measuring help you find out whether heat has changed the water in a pot on the stove?

Technology Visit www.eduplace.com/scp/ to find out more about heat.

Lesson 2

Where Does Light Come From?

Science and You
A lighthouse helps ships find their way in the dark.

Inquiry Skill
Ask Questions You can ask questions to learn more about the world around you.

What You Need

objects

paper

tape

flashlight

Investigate

Shine Light

Steps

1. Tape paper to a wall. Shine light on the paper.

2. **Observe** Hold one object between the flashlight and the paper.

3. **Record Data** Write or draw what you see.

4. **Predict** Tell which objects you think light will pass through. Repeat steps 2 and 3 for each object.

STEP 1

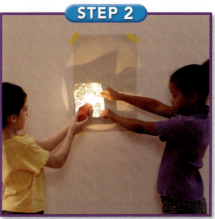

STEP 2

STEP 3

Think and Share

1. How did your predictions compare to what happened?

2. **Classify** Group the objects by how light passes through them. Explain your groups.

Investigate More!

Ask Questions Complete this sentence: I wonder if light will pass through ___. Predict what will happen. Then try it. Share your results.

Learn by Reading

Vocabulary
light
shadow

Reading Skill
Main Idea and Details

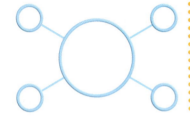

Light

You know that Earth gets heat from the Sun. Earth also gets light from the Sun. **Light** is a kind of energy that you can see.

Things other than the Sun give off light, too. Fires, candles, and matches are things that burn. They give off light and heat.

The Sun gives off light.

▲ nightlight

▲ fireworks

Light bulbs give off light. When you bend a glow stick, it gives off light. Even some living things give off light.

▶ **MAIN IDEA** What is light?

▲ firefly

Light and Shadows

Light can pass through some things but not others. Light passes through clear glass and clear plastic. It also passes through water and air.

What Light Passes Through

1 Light passes through.

2 Some light passes through.

3 No light passes through.

Other things stop some or all light from passing through. Wax paper and sunglasses block some light. Your body blocks all light. A dark shape called a **shadow** forms when something blocks light.

▶ **MAIN IDEA** What is a shadow?

The boy and the dog block light from the Sun.

Lesson Wrap-Up

1. **Vocabulary** What kind of energy can you see?

2. **Reading Skill** What are four things that give off light?

3. **Ask Questions** What else do you want to know about light and shadows?

Technology Visit www.eduplace.com/scp/ to find out more about light.

Lesson 3

How Is Sound Made?

Science and You
Many living things use sound to communicate.

Inquiry Skill
Observe You can look and listen to learn about something.

What You Need

goggles

rubber band

can

Investigate

Make Sounds

Steps

1. Stretch a rubber band around a can, across the open top. **Safety:** Wear goggles. Hold the rubber band carefully!

2. **Observe** Use your finger to pluck the rubber band. Look and listen closely.

3. **Record Data** Write about what you see and hear.

Think and Share

1. **Compare** How did the rubber band change when you plucked it?

2. **Infer** How do you think sound is made? Tell why.

Investigate More!

Solve a Problem Think of two ways to change the sound the rubber band makes. Then try them. Share your ways with the class.

F19

Learn by Reading

Vocabulary
sound
vibrates

Reading Skill
Draw Conclusions

Sound

Sound is a kind of energy that you can hear. Sound is made when something **vibrates**, or moves back and forth very fast. Many kinds of things vibrate and make sound—even you!

The space shuttle makes sound when it blasts off. ▶

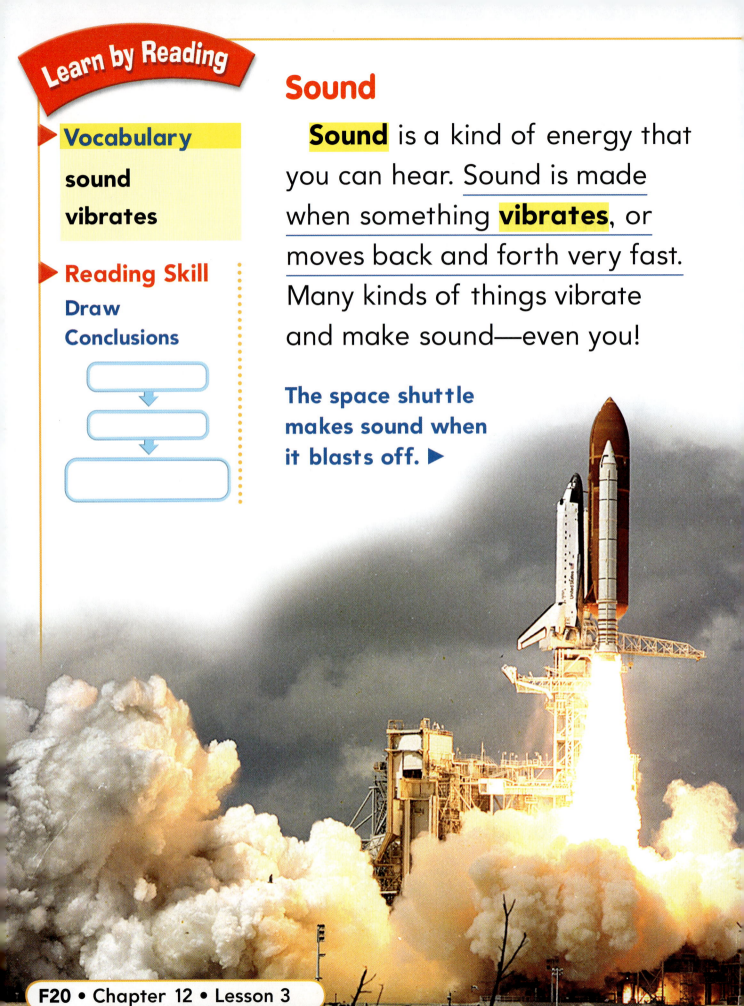

You make sound when you talk or sing. Sound happens when moving air makes parts inside your neck vibrate. Place your hand on the side of your neck as you talk. You can feel the parts vibrate.

▲ Birds make sounds when they sing.

▶ **DRAW CONCLUSIONS** What causes sound when a bird sings?

▼ Sound can be music.

Hearing Sound

A drum vibrates when you strike it. Something that vibrates makes air around it vibrate, too. Air that vibrates makes parts inside your ears vibrate. Then you hear sound.

▶ **DRAW CONCLUSIONS** How does the sound of a drum reach your ears?

Lesson Wrap-Up

❶ **Vocabulary** What is **sound**?

❷ **Reading Skill** How do you think a guitar string makes a sound?

❸ **Observe** If you see something vibrate, what will you hear?

🖥️ **Technology** Visit www.eduplace.com/scp/ to find out more about sound.

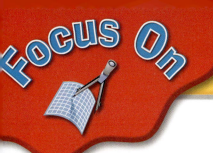

Focus On Technology READING LINK

Thump, Thump

A doctor uses a stethoscope to hear sounds inside your body. Part of the stethoscope vibrates when your heart beats. Vibrations go through tubes on the stethoscope to the doctor's ears.

Sharing Ideas

1. **Write About It** Draw a stethoscope. Write about how sound moves in it.
2. **Talk About It** Talk about questions that you can ask doctors about what they hear through stethoscopes.

Lesson 4

How Are Sounds Different?

Science and You
Sometimes people use sounds to make music.

Inquiry Skill
Use Data Compare what you learn to find patterns.

What You Need

5 jars

water

pencil

paper

Investigate

Different Sounds

Steps

1. Pour different amounts of water into four jars. Leave one jar empty.

2. **Observe** Tap the side of each jar with a pencil. Listen to the sounds.

3. **Record Data** Write letters to order the jars from the lowest sound to the highest sounds.

STEP 1

STEP 2

STEP 3

Think and Share

1. **Use Data** Which jar made the lowest sound? Which made the highest sound? How much water was in those jars?

2. **Infer** How does the amount of water affect the sound?

Investigate More!

Be an Inventor Hum a song. Use the jars to play the song. Add more jars and water if you need them. Then have a class concert.

Learn by Reading

Vocabulary

pitch
volume

Reading Skill
Compare and Contrast

Pitch and Volume

Not all sounds are the same. **Pitch** is how high or low a sound is. The faster something vibrates, the higher the sound it makes. Fast vibrations cause a high pitch. Slow vibrations cause a low pitch.

violin with high pitch ▼

bass with low pitch ▶

Volume is how loud or soft a sound is. Think about the sounds you make. When you whisper, you use a little energy to make a soft sound. When you yell, you use a lot of energy to make a loud sound.

▶ **COMPARE AND CONTRAST**
How is a high pitch different from a low pitch?

loud volume ▲

▼ soft volume

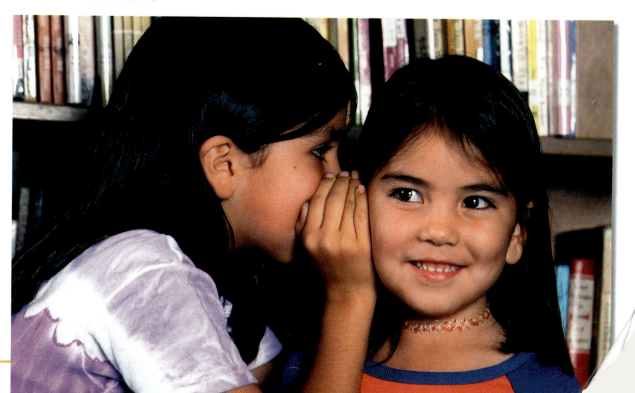

Sounds Keep You Safe

Some sounds are warnings that keep you safe. They warn you to get out of the way or to go to a safe place.

▲ Smoke alarms beep when something is burning.

Sirens warn drivers to get out of the way.

Lesson Wrap-Up

1. **Vocabulary** What is **volume**?
2. **Reading Skill** Compare loud and soft sounds.
3. **Use Data** What does how fast or slow something vibrates tell about pitch?

Technology Visit www.eduplace.com/scp/ to find out more about sound.

LINKS for Home and School

Math — Find a Sound

Work with four classmates. Give each classmate a bell. Put on a blindfold. Look at the picture to see how to stand.

When one classmate rings a bell, use the words **left**, **right**, **front**, or **back** to tell where you heard the sound.

Music — Change the Volume

How do you make the volume of music softer? Play one instrument. Then try to make a softer sound. Play another instrument. Again, try to make a softer sound. Tell what you did each time to make the volume softer.

Chapter 12 Review and Test Prep

Visual Summary

Energy sources give off heat, light, or sound.

Heat	Light	Sound
Energy that makes things warm	Energy that you can see	Energy that you can hear

Main Ideas

1. What are three things that give off heat? (pp. F8–F9)

2. Tell one way that energy causes change. (p. F10)

3. How are pitch and volume different? (pp. F26–F27)

4. What are two things that make sounds to keep you safe? (p. F28)

SAT 10 Practice

Vocabulary and Science Skills

Choose the correct answer.

5. Heat is a kind of ____.
   ○ change   ○ energy   ○ shade

6. Which forms when an object blocks light?
   ○ sunshine   ○ energy   ○ shadow

7. Sound is made when something ____.
   ○ is still   ○ listens   ○ vibrates

8. Which tells how loud or soft a sound is?
   ○ pitch   ○ volume   ○ noise

9. Which blocks all light?
   ○ water   ○ wax paper   ○ a dog

10. Which warms Earth's air, water, and land?
    ○ a fire   ○ a stove   ○ the Sun

Chapter 13

Moving Faster and Slower

Vocabulary Preview

force
push
pull
gravity
machine
speed
motion

force
A push or a pull is a force.

gravity
Gravity is a force that pulls objects toward Earth's center.

speed
Speed is how fast or slow something moves.

motion
Motion is moving from one place to another.

Lesson 1

What Makes Things Move?

Science and You
Simple machines can help you move heavy objects.

Inquiry Skill
Communicate Talk to others about what you observe and do.

What You Need

objects

paper and pencil

Investigate

How Things Move

Steps

1. Think of ways to make objects move. You might use one object to move another. See if you can make some things move in a curve.

STEP 1

2. **Record Data** Write how you moved each object.

STEP 2

3. **Communicate** Talk to others about what you observed.

STEP 3

Think and Share

1. What made each object move?
2. **Communicate** Talk about which objects were easier to move.

Investigate More!

Solve a Problem Some children want to play marbles. They need a flat surface. How can they use a marble to find the best place to play?

Learn by Reading

Vocabulary

force
push
pull
gravity
machine

Reading Skill

Cause and Effect

Pushes and Pulls

A push or a pull is a **force**. A force can make an object change its speed or direction. A **push** is a force that moves something away from you. A **pull** is a force that moves something closer to you.

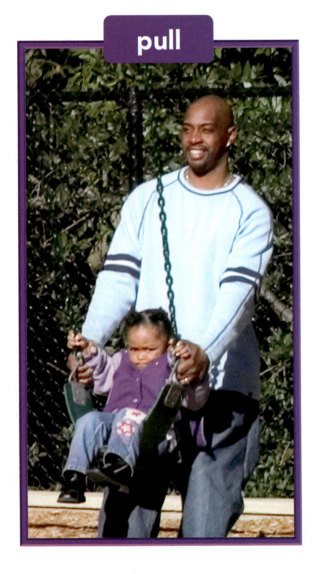

pull

push

Gravity is a force that pulls objects toward Earth's center. Objects fall to the ground when you drop them because gravity pulls them. Gravity makes you fall down when you trip.

🔴 **CAUSE AND EFFECT** What kind of force causes something to move away from you?

Machines That Help

A **machine** is a tool that makes some things easier to do. Ramps, levers, and pulleys are three kinds of machines. People use these machines to move things.

A hammer and a flip top are kinds of levers.

◀ A pulley makes lifting or moving objects easier.

A ramp makes it easier to roll things up or down. ▼

🟠 **CAUSE AND EFFECT** Why do people use machines?

Lesson Wrap-Up

1. **Vocabulary** What are two kinds of **force**?
2. **Reading Skill** What causes objects to move?
3. **Communicate** How would you explain to a friend what a machine does?

🔦 **Technology** Visit www.eduplace.com/scp/ to find out more about forces.

Lesson 2

What Things Move Fast and Slow?

Science and You
You probably move fast when you go down a hill and slow when you go up.

Inquiry Skill
Compare You can look for ways that objects move at different speeds.

What You Need

2 books

cardboard

toy car

tape

Investigate

Compare Distance

Steps

1. Make a ramp by placing cardboard on the edge of one book.

STEP 1

2. Let a car go from the top of the ramp. Put a piece of tape where the car stops.

STEP 2

3. **Experiment** Stack two books. Make a new ramp by placing cardboard at the edge of the top book. Repeat Step 2.

STEP 3

Think and Share

1. **Compare** Which time did the car travel farther?
2. **Infer** Why did the car travel farther that time?

Investigate More!

Experiment Take the car apart. Try each part on a ramp. Compare the distance each part travels with the distance the car traveled in Step 2.

F41

Learn by Reading

Vocabulary
speed

Reading Skill
Categorize and Classify

Speed

Speed is how fast or slow something moves. Some things move at a fast speed. An airplane flies fast. Juice can be poured fast. Some objects move at a slow speed. A caterpillar moves slowly. Honey drips slowly.

▶ **CLASSIFY** Name two things that move fast.

◀ fast

◀ slow

Compare Speeds

▲ **Different things move at different speeds.**

Slow Changes

Objects can move or change at different speeds. It is easy to see a soccer ball move fast when it is kicked. But some changes are so slow that they are hard to see.

The minute hand moves faster than the hour hand.

A plant grows so slowly that you cannot see it moving.

You cannot see plants and people grow while you watch. You can tell that they have grown if you measure them at different times.

▶ **CLASSIFY** What are some things that change slowly?

People grow slowly. ▶

Lesson Wrap-Up

1. **Vocabulary** What tells how fast or slowly an object moves?

2. **Reading Skill** Describe the speeds of a snail moving and a flower blooming.

3. **Compare** Which moves at a faster speed, a rabbit or a train?

Technology Visit www.eduplace.com/scp/ to find out more about speed.

F45

Focus On Readers' Theater

Fast Rides and Slow Lines

Cast
Mom, **Dad**, **Nikki**, and **James**

Dad: Who wants to ride the roller coaster?

Nikki: I do! It moves fast.

James: I do not! It is too fast. I want to go slow!

Dad: Then stand in line for the teacups ride. That line moves very slowly!

READING LINK

Mom: So do the teacups. I could push those teacups faster myself!

James: Let's race to the log ride. That is not too fast or too slow.

Nikki: Mom, Dad, speed up! Do you need to have me pull you?

James: Fast, slow. Push, pull. My head is spinning, and I am not even on a ride yet!

Nikki: Well then, this is a great amusement park!

Sharing Ideas

1. **Write About It** Compare the speeds of two things at the amusement park.
2. **Talk About It** What is the fastest thing you can think of? What is the slowest?

Lesson 3

What Makes Things Speed Up or Slow Down?

Science and You
You can use forces to make objects go faster or slower.

Inquiry Skill
Measure You can use a tool to find how much or how many.

What You Need

tape

toy car

paper-clip chain

Investigate

Change Motion

Steps

1. Use tape to mark a starting place. Place a car at the tape mark. Gently roll the car. Use tape to mark where the car stops.

2. **Measure** Use a paper-clip chain to measure how far the car went. Record your data.

3. Start again at the first tape mark. Try to roll the car farther than you did the first time. Repeat step 2.

STEP 1

STEP 2

STEP 3

Think and Share

1. **Compare** What did you do to change how far the car went?

2. **Infer** How does force change how objects

Investigate More!

Ask Questions What else can you do to change how the car moves? Finish the question: What would happen if I _____?

Learn by Reading

Vocabulary
motion

Reading Skill
Compare and Contrast

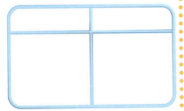

Motion

Motion is moving from one place to another. You can use force to change the motion of something. You can use a lot of force or a little force. You can stop motion, too.

▶ **COMPARE AND CONTRAST** How can you change motion?

The kicker changes the direction of the ball when she kicks it. The harder she kicks, the farther the ball goes.

Catching the ball stops its motion.

The player pushes the ball when he rolls it. The harder he rolls it, the faster the ball moves.

Moving Heavy Objects

Heavy objects are harder to move than light objects. You have to use more force to move a heavy object. Heavy objects are harder to stop, too.

heavy

light

Lesson Wrap-Up

1. **Vocabulary** What is **motion**?

2. **Reading Skill** Compare moving a heavy book with moving a light book.

3. **Measure** How many hands fit across your desk?

Technology Visit www.eduplace.com/scp/ to find out more about motion.

LINKS for Home and School

Math Direction and Position

Make word cards using the words below. First, pick a card. Then have a partner act out the word on the card. Say what your partner is doing.

to the left
to the right
away from
toward

under
above
inside
outside

Social Studies Around Town

Draw a picture to show ways that people move from one place to another in your town.

Chapter 13 Review and Test Prep

Visual Summary

Forces can change the speed and motion of things.

Forces			Speed		Motion	
Push	Pull	Gravity	Fast	Slow	Start	Stop

Main Ideas

1. What makes objects change speed or direction? (p. F36)

2. Name two machines and tell what they do. (pp. F38–F39)

3. Sometimes you cannot see something change. Tell why. (p. F44)

4. How can you change motion? (pp. F50–F51)

SAT 10 Practice

Vocabulary and Science Skills

Choose the correct answer.

5. Gravity is a force that ____.
   ○ lifts   ○ pulls   ○ pushes

6. Which tells how fast something is moving?
   ○ gravity   ○ motion   ○ speed

7. Tools that make things easier to do are ____.
   ○ forces   ○ machines   ○ gravity

8. A push or a pull is a ____.
   ○ force   ○ motion   ○ object

9. Which can move fastest?
   ○ train   ○ car   ○ rabbit

10. Which changes the motion of something?
    ○ force   ○ speed   ○ direction

Wrap-Up

Discover!

What is the fastest a human can run?

At the Olympics in 1996, a man ran 200 meters in 19.32 seconds. That's about 23 miles an hour. But compared to a cheetah, humans are slow. A cheetah can run three times as fast!

Go to **www.eduplace.com/scp/** to see animals and objects that move fast and slow.

Science and Math Toolbox

Using a Hand Lens H2
Using a Thermometer H3
Using a Ruler H4
Using a Calculator H5
Using a Balance H6
Making a Chart H7
Making a Tally Chart H8
Making a Bar Graph H9

Using a Hand Lens

A hand lens is a tool that makes objects look bigger. It helps you see the small parts of an object.

Look at a Coin

1. Place a coin on your desk.

2. Hold the hand lens above the coin. Look through the lens. Slowly move the lens away from the coin. What do you see?

3. Keep moving the lens away until the coin looks blurry.

4. Then slowly move the lens closer. Stop when the coin does not look blurry.

Using a Thermometer

A thermometer is a tool used to measure temperature. Temperature tells how hot or cold something is. It is measured in degrees.

Find the Temperature of Water

1. Put water into a cup.

2. Put a thermometer into the cup.

3. Watch the colored liquid in the thermometer. What do you see?

4. Look how high the colored liquid is. What number is closest? That is the temperature of the water.

Science and Math Toolbox

Using a Ruler

A ruler is a tool used to measure the length of objects. Rulers measure length in inches or centimeters.

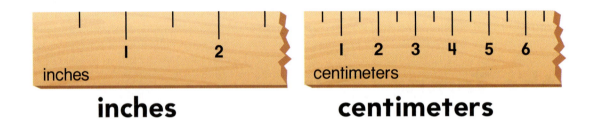

inches   centimeters

Measure a Crayon

1. Place the ruler on your desk.

2. Lay your crayon next to the ruler. Line up one end with the end of the ruler.

3. Look at the other end of the crayon. Which number is closest to that end?

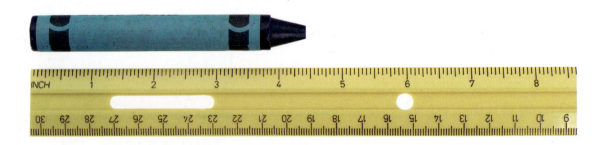

Using a Calculator

A calculator is a tool that can help you add and subtract numbers.

Subtract Numbers

1. Tim and Anna grew plants. Tim grew 5 plants. Anna grew 8 plants.

2. How many more plants did Anna grow? Use your calculator to find out.

3. Enter 8 on the calculator. Then press the − key. Enter 5 and press = .

What is your answer?

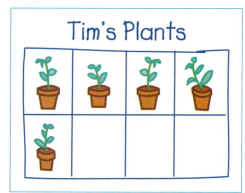

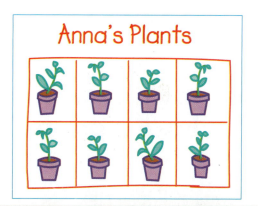

Using a Balance

A balance is a tool used to measure mass. Mass is the amount of matter in an object.

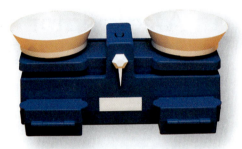

Compare the Mass of Objects

1. Check that the pointer is on the middle mark of the balance. If needed, move the slider on the back to the left or right.

2. Place a clay ball in one pan. Place a crayon in the other pan.

3. Observe the positions of the two pans.

Does the clay ball or the crayon have more mass?

Making a Chart

A chart can help you sort information, or data. When you sort data it is easier to read and compare.

Make a Chart to Compare Animals

1. Give the chart a title.

2. Name the groups that tell about the data you collect. Label the columns with the names.

3. Carefully fill in the data in each column.

Which animal can move in the most ways?

How Animals Move

Animal	How It Moves
fish	swim
dog	walk, swim
duck	walk, fly, swim

Science and Math Toolbox

Making a Tally Chart

A tally chart helps you keep track of items as you count.

Make a Tally Chart of Kinds of Pets

Jan's class made a tally chart to record the number of each kind of pet they own.

1. Every time they counted one pet, they made one tally.

2. When they got to five, they made the fifth tally a line across the other four.

3. Count the tallies to find each total.

How many of each kind of pet do the children have?

Kinds of Pets

cat	|||| ||
dog	|||| |||
hamster	|||

Making a Bar Graph

A bar graph can help you sort and compare data.

Make a Bar Graph of Favorite Pets

You can use the data in the tally chart on page H8 to make a bar graph.

1. Choose a title for your graph.

2. Write numbers along the side.

3. Write pet names along the bottom.

4. Start at the bottom of each column. Fill in one box for each tally.

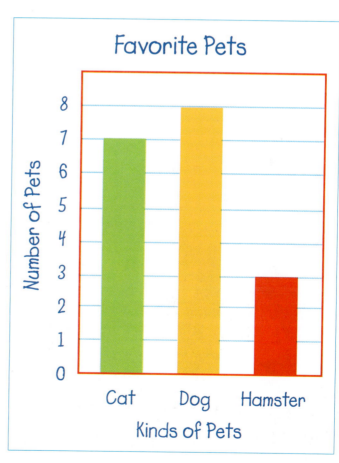

Which pet is the favorite?

Science and Math Toolbox

Health and Fitness Handbook

Health and Fitness Handbook

Are you healthy? You are if you:

- know how your body works.
- practice safe actions when you play.
- know how to stay well.
- are active every day.
- eat healthful foods.

Inside Your Body H12
Learn some of the body parts that let you run, think, and breathe.

Foods for Healthy Bones and Teeth H14
Find out which foods help keep bones and teeth strong.

Caring for Your Teeth H15
Brush and floss for healthy teeth.

Fun and Fit on the Playground H16
Find out how to make your body stronger as you play.

A Safe Bike H17
Are you safe on your bike? Find out.

Health and Fitness Handbook

Inside Your Body

Your body has many parts. All the parts work together.

Brain
Your brain helps you think. It controls all your other body parts.

Heart
Your heart pumps blood through your body. Your heart is about the size of your fist.

Lungs
Air goes in and out of your lungs. Your body needs air to stay alive.

Stomach
Your stomach helps change food so your body can use it.

Bones and muscles hold you up and help you move.

Bones

Your body has more than 200 bones. Some bones protect body parts.

- Your skull protects your brain.
- Your ribs protect your heart and lungs.
- There are 27 bones in each of your hands.

Muscles

Muscles move body parts.

- The muscles in your legs are large. They help you run, jump, and play.
- The muscles in your eyelids are tiny. They help you blink.
- Your heart is a muscle, too.

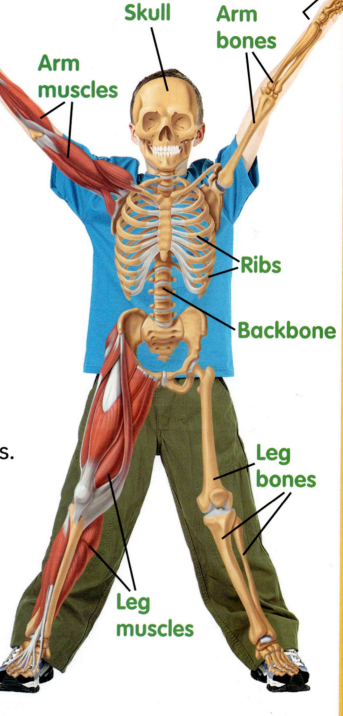

Foods for Healthy Bones and Teeth

Your body needs calcium. Calcium makes bones and teeth strong. Get the right amount of calcium by eating three of these foods every day!

Dairy Foods

- milk
- yogurt
- cheese

Foods With Calcium Added

- cereal bars
- wheat bread
- cereal
- juices
- tofu
- waffles

Other Foods

- spinach
- bok choy
- garbanzo beans
- almonds

These foods give you one serving of calcium.

calcium-added orange juice

breakfast bar

two burritos

macaroni and cheese

Caring for Your Teeth

You use your teeth to chew, talk, and smile.

Brush Twice Each Day

Brush the fronts.

Brush the backs.

Brush the tops.

Floss Once Each Day

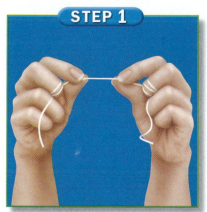
Wrap the floss and pull it tight.

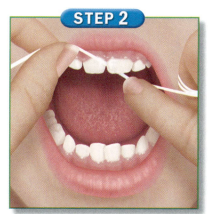
Slide the floss between teeth.

Dental Check-Ups

Dentists and dental hygienists clean and check your teeth. They use x-ray machines to check the hidden parts of teeth.

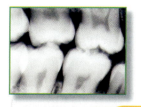

Fun and Fit on the Playground

Have Some Fun

It's time to go outside. How will you play today? Being active keeps your body fit. You feel good when you are fit. You can play hard and not get tired. You can bend your body in many ways.

Throw, kick, and catch.

Climb, skip, or swing.

Getting and Staying Fit

Do different activities to get fit and stay fit. Stretch before you start. Play hard. Then stretch again. Try these Fun and Fit ideas.

Have fun with friends.

A Safe Bike

You probably know how to ride a bike. Is your bike the right size? Your feet should reach the pedals easily. Your body should be above the bar when you stand.

Safety Equipment

Wear a helmet every time you ride. It should fit flat and protect your forehead. Pull the strap tight.

The right equipment can help keep you safe.

Picture Glossary

adult

A full-grown plant, animal, or person. (A46)

air pollution

Harmful things that get into the air. (C36)

amphibian

An animal that has wet skin with no hair, feathers, or scales. (A42)

attracts

Pulls toward. A magnet attracts iron and steel. (E20)

B

boulders

Very large rocks. (C15)

classify

Sort objects into groups that are alike in some way.

cloud

Many drops of water together. (D23)

communicate

Share what you learn with others by talking, drawing pictures, or making charts and graphs.

compare

Look for ways that objects or events are alike or different.

cone

The part of a pine tree where seeds grow. (A22)

desert

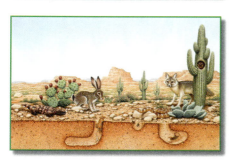

A place with very little water. (B42)

Picture Glossary

dissolve

To mix completely in water. (E52)

energy

Something that can cause change or do work. Heat is energy. (F8)

evaporate

To change from a liquid to a gas. (E46)

exercise

Movement that keeps your body strong. (A67)

experiment

Make a plan to collect data and then share the results with others.

F

fall

The season that follows summer. In fall, the weather gets cooler. (D34)

H20 • Glossary

fins
Body parts that help a fish move. (A34)

float
To stay on top of water. (E28)

flowers
The parts of plants that make seeds. (A11)

food
What living things use to get energy. (B16)

force
A push or a pull. A force can move an object. (F36)

forest
A place with many trees that grow close together. (B28)

freeze

To change from a liquid to a solid. A pond may freeze in winter. (E44)

gas

Matter that changes shape to fill all the space it is in. (E41)

gills

Parts of a fish that help it breathe under water. (A41)

gravity

A force that pulls objects toward Earth's center. Gravity pulls you down a slide. (F37)

heat

A kind of energy that makes things warm. (F8)

humus

Bits of rotting plants and animals in soil. (C24)

I

infant

A new baby. (A64)

infer

Use what you observe and know to tell what you think.

L

leaves

Parts of a plant that make food for the plant. (A10)

life cycle

The order of changes that happen in the lifetime of a plant or animal. (A22)

light

A kind of energy that you can see. (F14)

liquid

Matter that flows and takes the shape of its container. (E40)

living thing
Something that grows, changes, and makes other living things like itself. (B8)

lungs
Body parts that take in air. Birds and mammals use lungs to breathe. (A40)

M

machine
A tool that makes some things easier to do. A pulley is a machine. (F38)

magnet
An object that pulls iron and steel toward it. (E20)

magnify
To make something look larger. (E14)

mammal
An animal whose mother makes milk to feed her babies. (A40)

matter

What all things are made of. (E8)

measure

Use different tools to collect data about the properties of objects.

melt

To change from a solid to a liquid. Ice on a frozen pond will melt in spring. (E44)

mineral

A nonliving thing found in nature. A rock is made of one or more minerals. (C14)

mixture

Two or more kinds of matter put together. A sandwich is a mixture. (E50)

Moon

A space object close to Earth. (D58)

motion
Moving from one place to another. (F50)

natural resource
Something from Earth that people use. Water is a natural resource. (C8)

nonliving thing
Something that does not eat, drink, grow, and make other things like itself. (B10)

observe
Use tools and the senses to learn about the properties of an object or event.

ocean
A large body of salty water. (B34)

pitch

How high or low a sound is. A violin has a high pitch. (F26)

planet

A space object that moves around the Sun. (D48)

predict

Use what you know and patterns you observe to tell what will happen.

property

Anything that you learn about an object by using your senses. (E10)

pull

A force that moves something closer to you. (F36)

push

A force that moves something away from you. (F36)

record data

Write or draw to show what you have observed.

recycle

To take an object and make a new object from it. (C50)

reduce

To use less of something. (C52)

repel

To push away. Like poles of magnets repel each other. (E22)

reptile

An animal that has dry skin with scales. (A42)

reuse

To use something again. Watts Towers reuse tiles, seashells, and glass. (C48)

roots

The parts of a plant that take in water from the ground. (A9)

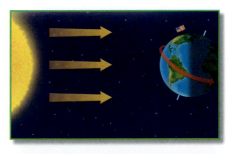

rotates

Spins. Day and night happen when Earth rotates. (D52)

season

A time of year that has its own kind of weather. (D28)

seed

The part of a plant that has a new plant inside it. (A11)

seedling

A young plant. (A22)

senses

Sight, smell, hearing, touch, and taste. You can see, smell, hear, feel, and taste popcorn. (A56)

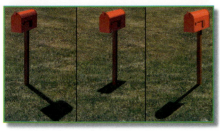

shadow

Something that forms when an object blocks light. (D68, F17)

shelter

A safe place for animals to live. (B20)

sink

To drop to the bottom of water. (E28)

sleep

Rest for body and mind. (A68)

soil

The loose top layer of Earth. (C24)

solid

Matter that has its own shape. (E38)

sound

A kind of energy that you can hear. Birds make sounds when they sing. (F20)

speed

How fast or slow something moves. Juice pours at a faster speed than honey. (F42)

spines

Sharp points on a cactus. (A14)

spring

The season that follows winter. Many baby animals are born in spring. (D28)

star

A space object that makes its own light. (D48)

stem

Part of a plant that connects the roots to the other plant parts. (A9)

summer

The season that follows spring. Summer is the warmest season. (D30)

Picture Glossary

Sun

The brightest space object in the day sky. (D47)

sunlight

Energy from the Sun. (B16)

 T

teen

A person between 13 and 19 years old. (A65)

temperature

How warm or cool something is. The temperature is cold when there is snow. (D14)

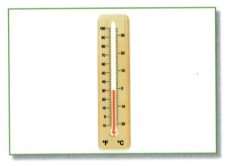

thermometer

A tool that measures temperature. (D14)

 U

Measurements of My Plants

Date	Measurement
October 1	3 inches
November 1	4 inches
December 1	$4\frac{1}{2}$ inches
January 1	5 inches
February 1	6 inches

use data

Use what you observe and record to find patterns and make predictions.

use models

Use something like the real thing to understand how the real thing works.

use numbers

Count, measure, order, or estimate to descibe and compare objects and events.

vibrates

Moves back and forth very fast. A drum vibrates when you strike it. (F20)

volume

How loud or soft a sound is. A whisper has soft volume. (F27)

water cycle

Water moving from Earth to the sky and back again. (D22)

Picture Glossary

water pollution

Harmful things that get into water. (C42)

weather

What the air outside is like. (D8)

weigh

To find out how heavy an object is. (E16)

wetland

A low area of land that is very wet. (B36)

wings

Body parts that help a bird fly through the air. (A34)

winter

The season that follows fall. Winter is the coldest season. (D36)

work together

Work as a group to share ideas, data, and observations.

Index

Adult, A29, A46, A65
Air
  in deserts, B42, B43
  floating and, E29, E56
  as a gas, E41
  heating of, F8
  light and, F16
  as natural resource, C8, C10, C11, C34–C37
  need of living things, B8, B13, B19
  pollution of, C31, C36–C37
  in soil, C24–C25
  sound and, F21–F22
Amphibian, A42
Animals, A28
  adult, A29, A46–A47
  air and, C34
  amphibians, A42
  birds, A34, A41, D29, F21
  body parts, A32–A35, A43, A58
  of deserts, B42–B44
  fish, A41
  food for, A17, A43, B16–B17, D31
  of forests, B28–B31
  life cycle, A46–A48
  mammal, A29, A40
  needs of, A10, B13, B16–B20, C11
  of oceans, B34–B35
  pollution and, C42
  reptiles, A29, A42
  seasons and, D29, D31, D35, D37
  soil and, C25
  of wetlands, B36–B37
Attract, E20–E25

Balance, E16
Biography
  Douglas, Marjory Stoneman, B38–B39
  Galilei, Galileo, D62–D63
Birds
  body parts, A34–A35, A41
  food for, A17
  hummingbird, A72
  spring and, D29
  wings of, A34–A35, A41
Boulders, C15

Cactus, A14, B44
Careers
  astronaut, D58
  environmentalist, B38–B39
  scientist, D62–D63
  writer, B38–B39
Cloud, D5, D23, D24–D25
Cone, A5, A22–A23

Day, D46–D47, D52–D53
Daylight, D28, D30, D34, D36
Desert, B25, B42–B44
Dissolve, E52
Douglas, Marjory Stoneman, B38–B39

Earth
  air, C8, C10, C11
  land, C8, C10–C11
  light from the Sun, F14
  Moon and, D60
  natural resources, C8–C11, C14–C17
  as a planet, D48
  rotation of, D52–D55, D67
  soil, C2, C24–C26
  Sun and, D47, F8
  water, C8–C9
Energy
  causes change, F10–F11
  from food, A66
  heat, F5, F8–F11
  light, F5, F14–F17
  sleep and, A68
  sound, F5, F20–F22, F27
Evaporate, E46
Exercise, A53, A60–A61, A66–A67

Fall, D34–D35, D38, E45
Fins, A29, A34, B35
Fire, B11
  heat from, F9–F11
  light from, F14
  water and, C41
Fish, A34, A41, B34–B35
Float, E28–E30, E56
Flower, A8, A11, A14, A18–A19

H35

Food
    of animals, A17, A43, D31
    need of living things, B5, B13, B16–B17
    of people, A16, A66, A69

Food chain, B17

Force, F33, F36–F39, F50–F52

Forest, B25, B28–B31

Freeze, E44–E45

Galilei, Galileo, D62–D63

Gas, E35, E41, E46

Gills, A41, B35

Gravity, F33, F37

Hand lens, E14–E15

Health and Safety
    Be Active, A60–A61
    Water Safety, C44–C45

Hearing, A56–A57, E8–E11, F22

Heat, F5, F8–F11

Humus, C5, C24

Infant, A53, A64

Inquiry Skills
    ask questions, A7, A31, A45, B15, B33, D21, F12, F13, F49
    be an inventor, D13, F25

    classify, A13, A38, A39, B6, B7, B33, C7, C13, C46, C47, D32, D33, E6, E7, F13
    communicate, A39, A45, A54, A55, A63, B26, B27, C13, C39, D26, D27, D33, E7, E37, E43, E49, F34, F35
    compare, A12, A13, A31, A45, A63, B7, B32, B33, B41, C13, C47, D20, D21, D33, D45, E13, E19, E36, E37, F7, F19, F40, F41, F49
    experiment, A21, A55, B41, C12, C13, C23, C33, C39, D27, D51, D57, D65, E19, E27, E43, F7, F41, F49
    infer, A30, A31, A63, B15, B27, B41, C7, C23, C33, C39, C47, D21, D27, D50, D51, E18, E19, E27, E43, F7, F19, F25, F41, F49
    measure, D12, D13, D21, E12, E13, F6, F7, F48, F49
    observe, A6, A7, A21, A31, A45, A63, B7, B14, B15, B27, C13, C22, C23, C33, D7, D21, D44, D45, D65, E13, E19, E27, E37, E43, E48, E49, F13, F18, F19, F25
    predict, D21, D27, D51, D64, D65, E19, E26, E27, E42, E43, E49, F13
    record data, A7, A13, A39, B7, B27, C33, C47, D6, D7, D13, D45, D65, E7, E19, E27, F7, F13, F19, F25, F35

    solve a problem, A39, C47, D33, E13, E37, F19, F35
    use data, C7, C32, C33, F24, F25
    use models, A20, A21, A44, A45, A55, C38, C39, D51, D56, D57
    use numbers, B40, B41, C6, C7, D57
    work together, A13, A62, A63, B7, B27, C7, D7, D45, E7, E49

Investigate
    cat's life cycle, A44–A45
    change motion, F48–F49
    classify animals, A38–A39
    classify objects, B6–B7, E6–E7
    collect pollution, C32–C33
    compare animals, B32–B33
    compare distance, F40–F41
    compare leaves, A12–A13
    compare matter, E36–E37
    compare rocks, C12–C13
    day and night, D50–D51
    different sounds, F24–F25
    float or sink, E26–E27
    grow plants, D26–D27
    hidden animals, A30–A31
    how things move, F34–F35
    land and water, C6–C7
    make a mixture, E48–E49
    make sounds, F18–F19
    measure heat, F6–F7

measure weather, D12–D13
model your body, A54–A55
Moon changes, D56–D57
observe a plant, A6–A7
observe plants, B14–B15
observe sky, D44–D45
observe soil, C22–C23
observe a tree, B26–B27
person's life, A62–A63
predict changes, E42–E43
record weather, D6–D7
shine light, F12–F13
sort your trash, C46–C47
Sun changes, D64–D65
use magnets, E18–E19
use plant models, A20–A21
use tools, E12–E13
water changes, D20–D21
waterwheel, C38–C39
wet or dry, B40–B41
what to wear, D32–D33

Leaves, A8, A10, A14, A18–A19, D34
Levers, F38
Life cycle
of animals, A46–A47, D29
of people, A64–A65
of plants, A22–A23

Light
in day, D46
energy of, F5, F14–F17
stars and, D48
Links for Home and School
art, E53
language arts, A49, B45, D69, E31
math, A25, A49, A69, B21, B45, C27, C53, D39, D69, E31, E53, F29, F53
music, A25, C27, F29
social studies, A69, B21, C53, D39, F53
Liquid, E35, E40, E52
adding solids to, E52
change to gas, E46
change to solid, E44–E45
Literature
Animal Disguises, A37
"City Rain," D19
"Ice Cycle," E47
"In a Winter Meadow," A36
Rain, D18
Living things, B5
of deserts, B42–B44
of forests, B28–B31
needs of, B8–B9, B16–B20
nonliving things or, B12–B13
of oceans, B34–B35
of wetlands, B36–B37
Lungs, A40–A41

Machine, F38–F39
Magnet, E5, E20–E23, E51
Magnify, E5, E14–E15

Mammal, A29, A40
Matter, E5
change in form, E44–E46
floating and sinking, E28–E30
forms of, E38–E41
length of, E17
magnets and, E20–E23
magnified, E14–E15
mixtures of, E50–E52
properties of, E10–E11, E16, E20–E23, E28–E30
senses and, E8–E11
weight of, E16, E29
Measuring tapes, E17
Melt, E35, E44–E45
Mineral, C5, C14–C17, C56
Mixture, E50–E52
Moon, D43, D48, D58–D61, D63, D67
Motion, F33, F36–F39, F50–F52

Natural resource, C5
air, C8, C10, C11, C34–C37
land, C8, C10
reuse, recycle, reduce, C48–C52
rocks and minerals, C14–C17
soil, C24–C27
water, C8–C9, C40–C43
Night, D48, D54–D55
Nonliving thing, B5, B10–B11
of deserts, B42–B43
of forests, B28–B29
living things or, B12–B13
of oceans, B34–B35

H37

Ocean, B25, B34–B35, C9, C40, C41
Oxygen, A10

Patterns, A25
  day and night, D52–D55
  seasons, D28–D31, D34–D38
  water cycle, D22–D23
People, A52
  air and, C34–C35
  body parts, A56–A59
  changes, F45
  exercise and, A60–A61, A66–A67
  food for, A16, B17
  growing and changing, A64–A65
  living things, B8–B10
  needs of, A66–A69
  pollution and, C36–C37, C42–C43
  senses of, A56–A57
  use of land, C10
  use of rocks, C16–C17
  use of water, C8, C40–C41
Pitch, F26
Planet, D43, D48
Plants, A4
  air and, C34, C37
  of deserts, B44
  eating, A16–A17, D31
  in forests, B28–B31
  growth, F45
  life cycle of, A22–A23
  needs of, B8, B16–B19, C24–C25
  parts of, A8–A11
  pollution and, C42
  seasons and, D28–D29, D31, D37
  sorting, A14–A15
  sunlight and, B16
  uses for, A18–A19
  of wetlands, B36–B37
Property
  floating and sinking, E28–E30
  length, E17
  magnets and, E21
  senses and, E10–E11
  weight, E16
Pull, F36
Pulleys, F38–F39
Push, F36

Rain
  clouds and, D11, D23–D25
  measuring, D16–D17
  plants and, D28
Rain gauge, D16–D17
Ramps, F38–F39
Readers' Theater
  Fast Rides and Slow Lines, F46–47
  Living or Nonliving, B12–B13
  Rock Stars, C18–C21
Reading in Science
  Dirt, C2–C3
  Energy: Heat, Light, and Fuel, F2–F3
  Over in the Meadow, B2–B3
  What Is the World Made Of?, E2–E3
  What's Alive?, A2–A3
  What Will the Weather Be?, D2–D3
Recycle, C31, C48, C50–C51
Reduce, C48, C52
Repel, E22–E23
Reptile, A29, A42
Reuse, C31, C48–C49
Rocks, C10, C14–C17, C18–C21, C56
Roots, A5, A8–A9, A14, A18–A19
Rotates, D52–D55
Ruler, E17

Salamanders, A42, A46–A47
Science inquiry, S6
Season, D5
  fall, D34–D35, D38
  pattern of, D38
  spring, D28–D29, D38
  summer, D30–D31, D38
  winter, D36–D38
Seed, A5, A11, A14, A18–A19, A22–A23
Seedlings, A22–A23
Senses, A53, A56–A57, E8–E11
Shadow, D68, D69, F17
Shape
  floating and sinking and, E29–E30
  gases, E41
  liquids, E40
  solids, E39
Shells, B48
Shelter, B5, B20
Sight, A56–A57, E8–E11
Sink, E5, E28–E30, E56
Sky
  in day, D46–D47, D52–D53
  at night, D48–D49, D54–D55

Sleep, A68
Sleet, D23
Smell, A56–A57, E8–E11
Snow, D25, D36–D37
Soil, C2, C5, C24–C26
Solid, E35, E38–E39
   in liquids, E52
   melting, E35, E44–E45
   mixtures of, E50–E52
Sound
   as energy, F5, F20–F22
   pitch, F26
   and safety, F28
   vibrations, F20–F22, F26
   volume, F5, F27
Space, B13, B18–B19
Speed, F33, F42–F45, F56
Spines, A5, A14
Spring, D28–D29, D38, E45
Star, D43, D47, D48, D67
Stem, A8, A9, A18–A19
Summer, D30–D31, D38
Sun, D43
   day and, D47, D52–D53
   Earth and, D66–D68
   heat from, F8, F10
   light from, F14
   Moon and, D59
   night and, D48, D54–D55
   shadows and, D68, F17
   water cycle and, D22
Sunlight, B16

Taste, A56–A57, E8–E11
Technology, S11
   Mighty Magnets, E24–E25
   Plant Power!, A18–A19
   Thump, Thump!, F23
Teen, A53, A65

Temperature, D14–D15
Thermometer, D5, D14–D15
Tools
   balance, E16
   hand lens, E14–E15
   machines, F38–F39
   for measuring weather, D14–D17
   rulers and measuring tapes, E17
   thermometer, D5, D14–D15
Touch, E8–E11
Trees, A14, C10
   forests, B25, B28–B31
   life cycle of, A22–A23
   uses for, A18

Vibrate, F20–F22, F26
Volume, F5, F27

Water, C40–C43
   change to gas, E46
   change to solid, E44–E45
   in clouds, D5, D23
   cycle, D22–D23
   deserts and, B25, B42
   fish, A41
   heating of, F8
   as natural resource, C8–C9
   need of living things, B13, B18–B19
   in oceans, B25, B34, C9
   pollution of, C31, C42–C43
   rain, D11, D16, D23–D25, D28
   soil and, C24, C25, C26
   in wetlands, B25, B36
Water cycle, D22–D23
Weather, D5
   changes, D10–D11
   clouds and, D24–D25
   in fall, D34–D35
   kinds of, D8–D11
   in spring, D28–D29
   in summer, D30–D31
   tools to measure, D14–D17
   in winter, D36–D37
Weigh, E16, E29
Wetland, B25, B36–B37, B38–B39
Windsock, D16
Wind vane, D16
Wings, A34–A35, A41
Winter, D36–D38, E45

Credits

Permission Acknowledgements

TRO © Copyright 1956 (Renewed), 1958 (Renewed), 1970 (Renewed), and 1972 (Renewed) Ludlow Music, Inc., New York, N.Y. Used by Permission. Excerpt from The Latest Look from Animal Disguises, by Belinda Weber. Copyright © 2004 Kingfisher Publications Plc. Reprinted by permission of Kingfisher Publications Plc, an imprint of Houghton Mifflin Company. Excerpt from In A Winter Meadow from The Frogs Wore Red Suspenders, by Jack Prelutsky. Copyright © 2002 by Jack Prelutsky. Reprinted by permission of HarperCollins Publishers. Excerpt from What's Alive?, by Kathleen Weidner Zoehfeld, illustrated by Nadine Bernard Westcott. Text copyright © 1995 by Kathleen Weidner Zoehfeld. Illustrations copyright © 1995 by Nadine Bernard Westcott. Reprinted by permission of HarperCollins Publishers. Excerpt from Over in the Meadow, by Ezra Jack Keats. Copyright © 1971 by Ezra Jack Keats. Copyright © renewed 1999 by Martin Pope, Executor of Ezra Jack Keats. Illustrations copyright © assigned to Ezra Jack Keats Foundation. Reprinted by permission of the Ezra Jack Keats Foundation and of Viking Children's Books, a division of Penguin Young Readers Group, a member of Penguin Group (USA) Inc., 345 Hudson Street, New York, NY 10014. All rights reserved. Excerpt from Dirt, by Steve "The Dirtmeister" Tomacek, illustrated by Nancy Woodman. Text copyright © 2002 by Stephen M. Tomacek. Illustrations copyright © 2002 by Nancy Woodman. Reprinted by permission of National Geographic Society. Excerpt from *City Rain* from *Taxis and Toadstools*, by Rachel Field. Copyright © 1926 by Doubleday, a division of Random House, Inc. Reprinted by permission of Random House Children's Books, a division of Random House, Inc. *Rain*, by Manya Stojic. Copyright © 2000 by Manya Stojic. Reprinted by permission of Crown Publishers, an imprint of Random House Children's Books, a division of Random House, Inc. Excerpt from *What Will the Weather Be?*, by Lynda DeWitt, illustrated by Carolyn Croll. Text copyright © 1991 by Lynda DeWitt. Illustrations copyright © 1991 by Carolyn Croll. Reprinted by permission of HarperCollins Publishers. *Ice Cycle*, by Mary Ann Hoberman, from *Once Upon Ice and Other Frozen Poems*, selected by Jane Yolen, illustrated by Jason Stemple. Text Copyright © 1997 by Mary Ann Hoberman. Photographs copyright © 1997 by Jason Stemple. Text reprinted by permission of Gina Maccoby Literary Agency. Photographs published by Wordsong, Boyds Mills Press, Inc. Reprinted by permission. Excerpt from What is the World Made of?, by Kathleen Weidner Zoehfeld, illustrated by Paul Meisel. Text copyright © 1998 by Kathleen Weidner Zoehfeld. Illustrations copyright © 1998 by Paul Meisel. Reprinted by permission of HarperCollins Publishers. Excerpt from Big Freeze, by Catherine Chambers. Copyright © 2002 by Reed Educational & Professional Publishing. Reprinted by permission of Harcourt Education. Excerpt from Energy, Heat, Light, and Fuel, by Darlene Stille, illustrated by Sheree Boyd. Copyright © 2004 by Picture Window Books. Reprinted by permission of Picture Window Books.

Cover

(Seal pup) (Spine) Digital Vision/Getty Images. (Back cover seal) Daniel J. Cox/Getty Images. (Ice) Royalty-Free/CORBIS.

Photography

A00 Bob Rozinski/Dancing pelican. **A1** Len Kaufman Photography. **A4–A5** (bkgd) Yoshio Sawaraqi/getty images. **A5** (t) Phil Degginger/Ed Degginger Photography. (bc) Christine M. Douglas/DK Images. **A6** (bl) Hans Reinhard/Bruce Coleman, Inc. **A6–A7** (bkgd) Birgit Koch/Alamy. **A8** Phil Degginger/Color-Pic, Inc. **A9** (br) Rich Iwasaki/ Stone/Getty Images; (tr) Steve Gorton/DK Images. **A10** (bl) Matthew Ward/DK Images. (cl) Scott Camazine. (br) Heather Weston/ Botanica/Getty Images. (c) Henry Beeker/Alamy. (tr) Peter Gardner/DK images. **A12** (bl) Rita Maas/ Foodpix. **A12–A13** (bkgd) Michael P. Gadomski/Photo Researchers, Inc. **A16** (b) David Young-Wolff/Photoedit, Inc. (cr) Clay Perry/Corbis. **A17** ©E.R. Degginger/Color-Pic, Inc. **A18–A19** (bkgd) Robert Holmgren/ Stone/Getty Images. **A19** (tr) Corbis; (tcl) Andy Crawford/DK Images. (tcr) Susanna Price/DK Images; (bcl) David Murray/DK Images. (bcr) Steve Gorton/DK Images. (bl) John Foxx/Alamy Images; (br) DK Images. (tl) Siede Preis/Photodisc/Getty Images. **A20** (bl) Matthew Ward/DK Images. **A20–A21** (bkgd) Balfour Studios/Alamy Images. **A24** (tl) Darrell Gulin/DRK Photo. (c) John Gerlach/dembinsky Photo Associates. **A26** ©Phil Degginger/Ed Degginger Photography. **A28–A29** (bkgd) Johnny Johnson/AlaskaStock.com. **A29** (t) Masa Ushioda/Stephen Frink Collection/Alamy Images; (tc) Juniors Bildarchiv/Alamy; (bc) Suzanne L. & Joseph T. Collins/Photo Researchers, Inc. (b) © R.R. Degginger/Color Pic, Inc. A30 (bl) © E.R. Degginger/Color Pic, Inc. (tr) S Solum/ Photo link/Photodisc/Getty Images. **A30–A31** (bkgd) Ingo Arndt/Foto Natura/ Minden Pictures. **A32** Dave King/DK Images. **A33** (tc) Bach/Zefa/ Masterfile; (tl) Nigel Dennis/Photo Researchers, Inc. (bc) ©E.R. Degginger/Color Pic, Inc. (tr) Michael DeYoung/AlaskaStock.com. (bl) ©E.R. Degginger/Color Pic, Inc.; (bl) Tom Brakefield/Corbis. **A34–A35** (b) Masa ushioda/ Stephen Frink Collection/Alamy Images. **A35** (tr) Joe Mcdonald/Corbis. (tl) Alan & Sandy Carey/ Photo Researchers, Inc. **A36** (b) Gail Shumway / Taxi/Getty Images. **A37** Stephen Krasemann /Stone/ Getty Images. **A38** (bl) Laura Riley/ Bruce Coleman, Inc. **A38–A39** (bkgd) Greg Dimijian/ Photo Researchers, Inc. **A40** Juniors Bildarchiv/ Alamy. **A41** (tr) Larry Ditto/Bruce Coleman, Inc. (b) Larry Lipsky/DRK Photo. **A42** (tl) Suzanne L. & Joseph T. Collins/ Photo Researchers, Inc. (bl) Darren Maybury; Eye Ubiquitous/Corbis; (br) Georgette Douwma/ Photographer's Choice/Getty Images. **A43** (l) Jerry Young/D K Images. (r) Digital Vision/Getty Images. **A44–A45** Alan & Sandy Carey/Photo Researchers, Inc. **A46** ©E.R. Degginger/Color Pic, Inc. **A46–A47** (bkgd) George Herben/AlaskaStock.com *A47* (bl) ©E.R. Eegginger/Color Pic, Inc.; (br) Suzanne L. Collins/Photo Researchers, Inc. A48 Ardea. **A50** (l) Alan & Sandy Carey/Photo Researchers, Inc. (cl) Larry Ditto/Bruce Coleman, Inc. (c) Larry Lipsky/DRK Photo. (cr) ©E.R. Degginger/Color Pic, Inc. (r) Skip Moody/Dembinsky Photo Associates, Inc. **A52** (bkgd) David Zelick/Imagebank/Getty Images. **A53** (t) Larry Ditto/Bruce Coleman, Inc. (tc) Rommel/Masterfile. (bc) Pierre Arsenault/Masterfile. (b) Ted Wood/Imagebank/Getty Images. **A54–A55** (b) Olivier Ribardiere/Taxi/Getty Images. **A57** (tr) Phil Degginger/Color Pic, Inc. (tl) Chris King/DK Images. (cr) C Squared Studios/Photodisc/Getty Images. **A58** Ryan McVay/ Photodisc/Getty Images. **A59** (r) Steve Shott/DK Images. (l) Jose Luis Pelaez, Inc./Corbis. **A62** (bl) Simon Taplin/Asia Images Group. (frame) Image Farm Inc. **A62–63** (bkgd) Photo 24/Brand X Pictures/Alamy. **A64** (bl) Rommel/Masterfile. (bc) DK Images. (br) Corbis. **A65** (bl) Pierre Arsenault/Masterfile. (bc) Ryan Mcvay/ Photodisc/Getty Images. (br) Rubberball/Alamy Images. **A67** Richard hutchings/Photo Researchers, Inc. **A68** Myrleen Ferguson Cate/Photo Edit Inc. **A70** (r) Myrleen Ferguson Cate/Photo Edit Inc. (l) Carlos Davila/ Superstock. **A72** Dominique Braud/Dembinsky Photo Associates, Inc. **B00** James D. Watt/Ocean Stock. **B1** Doug Perrine/Seapics. **B4–B5** Bermes/LAIF/Aurora. **B5** (bc) BananaStock/Picturequest. (b) Tom & Pat Leeson/Photo Researchers, Inc. (t) Eric Crichton / Bruce Coleman/ Picturequest. (tc) C Squared Studios / Photodisc/Getty Images. **B6** (bl) Brian Sytnyk/Masterfile. (t) Photospin. **B6–B7** (bkgd) Arthur S. Aubry/ Stone/Getty Images. **B8** (bc) Eric Crichton / Bruce Coleman/Picturequest. **B8–B9** (bkgd0 Ty Allison/Taxi/Getty Images. **B10** (br) Geri Engberg/The Image Works. (tc) Alan Pitcairn/Grant Heilman Photography. **B11** Norma Zuniga/Getty Images. **B14** (bl) Robert Lubeck/Animals Animals. **B14–B15** (bkgd) Kunst & Scheidulin/Premium/Panoramic Images. **B16** Liang Zhuoming/Corbis. **B17** (bc) J. H. Robinson/Photo Researchers, Inc. (br) Richard R. Hansen/Photo Researchers, Inc. (bl) Mark Gibson/Gibson Stock Photography. (tr) Arthur Morris/Corbis. (inset sun) SuperStock. **B18** (b) Steve Bloom/Taxi/Getty Images. (tr) Fotopic/Omni-Photo Communication. **B19** (b) Gerard Lacz/Animals Animals. (tr) Michael Boys/Corbis. **B20** (cr) Rick Sammon/Bruce Coleman Inc. (t) Tom & Pat leeson/Photo Researchers, Inc. (b) Robert Brenner/Photo Edit, Inc. **B24–B25** (bkgd) Gregory G. Dimijian/Photo Researchers, Inc. **B25** (t) Peter Griffith/Masterfile. (tc) Garry Black/Mastefile. (bc) Ace Stock Limited/ Alamy. (b) F. Damm/Masterfile. **B26** (bl) S. Nielsen/DRK Photo. **B26–B27** (bkgd) J. David Andrews/Masterfile. **B29** Arco/P. Wegner/Alamy. **B30** (c) Tom & Pat Leeson/DRK Photo. (t) Joe McDonald/DRK Photo. (b) RO-MA Stock/Index Stock. **B31** (t) M. Fogden/Bruce Coleman. (b) Lynn M. Stone/ DRK Photo. **B32** (bl) Doug Perrine/DRK Photo. **B32–B33** (bkgd) M. Timothy O'Keefe/Bruce Coleman. **B36** Jerry Young/DK Images. **B38** (tr) Kevin Fleming/Corbis. **B38–39** (bkgd) Jim steinberg/Photo Researchers, Inc. **B39** (tr) Savid Muench/Corbis. (bl) Mark Newman/Photo Researchers, Inc. **B40** (bl) ©E. R. Degginger/Color-Pic, Inc. **B40–B41** (bkgd) Bill Brooks/Masterfile. **B43** DK images. **B44** Linda Van Wijk/ MAsterfile. **B48** (l) Franklin Viola/Animals Animals. (c) Maresa Pryor/ Animals Animals. (r) G.I. Bernard/Photo Researchers, Inc. **C00** Tom Bean/DRK Photo. **C1** Tom Bean/DRK Photo. **C4–C5** (bkgd) Mark Newman/Bruce Coleman. **C5** (t) ©Dwight Kuhn/Dwight Kuhn Photography. (b) Gary Retherford/Photo Researchers, Inc. (tc) Harry Taylor/DK Images. **C6** (bl) D. Hurst/Alamy. **C6–C7** (bkgd) Mark Windom/ Index Stock. **C10** (tl) ©E.R. Degginger/Color Pic, Inc. (cl) ©E.R. Degginger/Color Pic, Inc. (cr) Dave King/DK Images. (tr) Wolfgang Kaehler/Corbis. **C11** Paul Barton/Corbis. **C12** (bl) ©E. R. Degginger/ Bruce Coleman, Inc. **C12–C13** (bkgd) S. Solum/Photolink/Getty images. **C14** (r) DK Images. **C14** (c) ©E.R. Degginger/Color Pic, Inc. (l) Cherles D. Winters/Photo Reasearchers. **C15** (tcr) DK Images. (l) Andreas Einsiedel/ DK images. (b) © E. R Degginger/Dembinsky Photo Associates. (tr) Stephen J Krasemann/Drk photo. (cr) Harry Taylor/DK Images. **C16** (br) Ben Johnson/ Science Photo Library/Photo Researchers, Inc. (tcr) Harry Taylor/DK images. (tr) Colin Keates/DK images. (tcl) DK Images. (tl) Superstock. (bcl) Charles d. Winters/Photo Researchers, Inc. (bl) Jack Sullivanq/Alamy Images. **C17** (r) Adrian Muttitt/Alamy Images. (l) Stphen J Krasemann/DRK Photo. **C22** (bl) S.L. Francisco Ontanon/The Image Bank/Getty Images. **C22–C23** (bkgd) Andreas Stirnberg/The Image Bank/Getty Images. **C25** (l) © Dwight Kuhn/Bruce Coleman, Inc. (r) Holt Studios/Nigel Cattlin/Photo Researchers, Inc. **C26** (r) Wayne Lawler/ Photo Researchers, Inc. (l) James Randklev/ChromoSohm Media Inc./ Photo Researchers, Inc. **C28** (bl) Gary Black/Masterfile. (tr) ©E. R. Degginger Color Pic, Inc. (tl) Mark Windom/Index stock. **C30–C31** (bkgd) Richard Levine/Alamy Images. **C31** (t) Michelle D. Bridwell/Photo Edit, Inc. (tc) Ken Graham/Bruce Coleman Inc. (b) Eric Fowke/Photo Edit, Inc. **C32–C33** (bkgd) Photri. **C34** Comstock Images/Getty Images **C35** (tr) Jack W. Dykinga/Bruce Coleman, Inc. (b) Lawrence migdale/Photo Researchers, Inc. **C36** (t) Michelle D. Bridwell/Photo Edit, Inc. (b) Jeff Greenberg/Photo Edit, Inc. **C37** Steve Helber/AP Wide World Photo. **C38** (bl) Cathy Melloan Resources/Photo Edit, Inc. **C38–C39** (bkgd) C. C. Lockwood/DRK Photo. **C40** (bl) Myrleen Ferguson Cate/Photo Edit, Inc. (r) SW productions/Getty images. **C41** (bl) Doug Martin/Photo Researchers, Inc. (tr) David Schmidt/Masterfile. (br) Wernher Krutein/ Photovault. **C42** (b) Ken Graham/Bruce Coleman, Inc. (cl) Johnathan Nourok/Photo Edit Inc. **C43** © Jonathan Nourok/Photo Edit. **C44** (br) Chris Coxwell/Corbis. **C46** (bl) Comstock Images. **C46–C47** (bkgd) Michael Wickes/Bruce Coleman, Inc. **C48** (bc) Patrick Palunbo/Wildlife Creations International USA. **C49** (t) Michael Newman/Photo Edit, Inc. **C50** (bl) Eric Fowke/Photo Edit, Inc. (br) ©E.R. Degginger/Color Pic, Inc. **C51** (tr) Michael newman/Photo Edit, Inc. (cr) Michael D. L. Jordan/ Dembinsky Photo Associates, Inc. (cl) Dennis MacDonald/Photo Edit, Inc. (b) © Photo Courtesy of Nike, Inc. **C54** (rc) Eric Fowke/Photo Edit, Inc. (l) C. C. Lockwood/DRK Photo. **C56** (l) Mark A. Scneider/Dembinsky Photo Associates, Inc. (c) Mark A. Scneider/Dembinsky Photo Associates, Inc. (r) © E.R. Degginger/Dembinsky Photo Associates, Inc. **D00** Adam Jones Photography. **D1** (b) S. Neilsen/DRK Photo. **D4–D5** (bkgd) Alan Schein Photography/Corbis **D5** (t) Ariel SKelley/Corbis. (bc) Tom BEan/DRK Photo. (bl) © E. R. Degginger/Color Pic, Inc. (tl) David Carriere/Index Stock Images. (br) Leonard Lee Ruell/Earth Scenes. (tr) George E. Jones 111/Photo Researchers, Inc. **D6** (bl) Ariel Skelley/Corbis. **D6–D7** (bkgd) Stephen St John/ National Geographic/Getty Images. **D8** Michael Newman/Photo Edit, Inc. **D9** (r) Ariel Skelley/Corbis. (l) Douglas Peebles/ Corbis. **D10** © Copyright 2001 Cynthia Malaran http://www.malaran.com from the website http://www.watchingthechanges.com All Rights Reserved. **D11** Robert Glusic/Photodisc/Getty Images. **D12** (bl) Robert Holmes/Corbis. **D12–D13** (bkgd) Burgess Blevins/Getty Images. **D14** Jeff Cadge/ The Image Bank/Getty Images. **D15** AJA Productions/ The Image Bank/Getty Images. **D16** (br) Jeff Grennberg/Photo Edit, Inc. (bl) David Young-Wolff/Photo Edit, Inc. **D17** (t) David Young-Wolff/ Photo Edit, Inc. (cr) Tony Freeman/Photo Edit, Inc. **D20–D21** (bkgd) Craig Tuttle/Corbis **D22–D23** (bkgd) Jim Steinberg/Photo Researchers, Inc. **D24** (c) Royalty-free/Corbis. **D24–D25** (bkgd) Terry Eggers/ Panoramic Images. **D25** (tl) Tom Bean/DRK Photo. (cr) Brock May/Photo Researchers Inc. **D26** (bl) Kim Taylor and Jane burton/DK images **D26–D27** (bkgd) Peter Adams Photography/Alamy Images **D28** Peter Dean/ Stone/Getty Images **D29** (bl) © Dwight Kuhn. (bc) Bob Jensen/Bruce Coleman Inc. (br) Dynamic Graphics Group/Creatas/Alamy Images. (tr) Julie Habel/Corbis. **D30** (b) Ariel Skelley/Corbis. (tl) Ed Young/Corbis. **D31** Premium Stock/Corbis. **D32** (bl) Siede Preis/ Photodisc/Getty Images. **D32–D33** (bkgd) Julio Lopez Saguar/Photonica. **D34** Ron Chapple/Thinkstock/Getty Images. **D35** (br) © Dwight Kuhn. (t) William h. Mullins/Photo Researchers, Inc. **D36** (bl) Steve Skjold/Photo Edit, Inc. **D37** Thomas Mangelsen/Minden Pictures **D38** (b) © E.R Degginger/ Color Pic, Inc. (r) Leonard Lee Ruell/Earth Scenes. (t) George E. Jones 111/Photo Researchers, Inc. (l) David Carriere/Index Stock Imagery. **D42–D43** (bkgd) Paul & Linda Marie Ambrose/Getty Images. **D43** (t) Gerard Lacz/Animals Animals. (tc) Nora Good/MAsterfile. (bc) Corbis. **D44** (bl) Raymond Tercafs/Bruce Coleman Inc. **D44–D45** (t) Don Farrall/ Photodisc/Getty Images. (b) Terry Thompson/Panoramic Images. (c) Dallas and John Heaton/Alamy Images. **D46** D. Robert & Lorri Franz/Corbis. **D47** (b) E. R. Degginger/Bruce Coleman Inc. (tr) GERARD LACZ/Animals Animals. **D48–D49** B.a.e. Inc./Alamy Images. **D50** (bl) Rettinghaus/Zefa/Masterfile. **D50–D51** (bkgd) Bill Brooks/ Masterfile. **D56** (bl) S. neilsen/DRK Photo. **D56–D57** (bkgd) Chris Cook/ Photo Researchers, Inc. **D58–D59** NASA/Bruce Coleman inc. **D60** (r) S. Neilsen/DRK photo. **D60–D61** (bkgd) Taxi/Getty Images. **D61** (l) S. Neilsen/DRK photo. (r) S. Neilsen/DRK photo. **D62** (tr) Bettmann/Corbis. (frame) Image Farm. **D62–D63** (bkgd) Nora Good/Masterfile. (b) Jim Sugar/Corbis. **D63** (c) Corbis. **D64** (bl) Marc Epstein/DRK Photo. **D64–D65** (bkgd) Michael Thompson/Animals Animals. **D65** (t bkgd) Martien Mulder/Stone/Getty Images. (b bkgd) Martien Mulder/Stone/Getty Images. **D66** (bl) Myrleen Ferguson Photo Edit, Inc. (br) Eric Fowke/ Photo Edit, Inc. **D67** (bl) Ariel Skelley/Corbis. (bc) Jeff Zaruba / Stone/ Getty Images. (br) DiMaggio/Kalish/Corbis. **D72** (l) David Stoecklein/ Corbis. **D72** (c) Randy Faris/Corbis. **D72** (r) Larry Gilpin/ Stone/Getty Images. **E1** Michele Stapleton/Michele Stapleton Photography. **E4–E5** (bkgd) Roy Morsch/Corbis. **E5** (tc) Robert George Young/Masterfile. (bc) C. Sagel/Masterfile. (t) Image Source/Alamy Images. **E08** Jade Lee/ Asia Images/Getty Images. **E6–E7** (bkgd) Peter Christopher/Masterfile. **E9** (c) Dave King/Dk Images. (r) Steve Shott/DK Images. **E10** (tr) Image Source/Alamy Images. (bl) Brand X Pictures/Getty Images. **E11** (bl) Corbis. (tl) Spencer Jones/ Foodpix/getty Images. (tr) Dave King/DK Images. (br) Dk Images. **E12–E13** (bkgd) Valerie Simmons/Masterfile. **E17** Martin Hanke/ Bildagentur Franz Waldhaeusl/Alamy Images. **E26** (bl) Dynamic Graphics/Picturequest. **E30** (br) Sie de Preis/ Photodisc/ Getty images. (bl) Siedie Preis/ Photodisc/Getty Images. **E34–E35** (bkgd) Kwame Zikomo/Age FotoStock America Inc. **E35** (t) GK & Vikki Hart/ Getty Images. (b) Christina Kennedy/photo edit inc. (tc) Steve Cole/ Getty images. (tc) Dynamic Graphics/Creatas. **E36–E37** (bkgd) JC Carton/Bruce Colman Inc. **E42** (bl) Stephen Shepard/Alamy Images. **E42–E43** (bkgd) Pekka, Parviainen/Photo Researchers, Inc. **E44** Michael Newman/Photo Edit, Inc. **E45** (t) Stephen G. Maka/DRK Photo. (c) Stephen G. Maka/DRk Photo. (b) Stephen G. Maka/DRK photo. (t) Chee Meng Ng/Chee Meng Ng Photography. **E46** (c) Chee Meng Ng/Chee Meng Ng Photography. (br) Daniel Barillot/Masterfile. **E47** Jason Stenple. **E53** (br) Adam Woolfitt/Alamy. **F00** Jeff Greenberg/The Image Works. **F1** Baby Face/PictureQuest. **F4–F5** (bkgd) Jeff Hunter/The Image Bank/Getty Images. **F5** (t) Daniel Barillot/Masterfile. (tc) Harald Sund/The Image Bank/Getty Images. (b) Michael Newman/Photo Edit, Inc. **F6–F7** (bkgd) Goodshot/Alamy Images. **F8** Richard T. Nowitz/ Corbis. **F9** (tr) Alchemy/Alamy images. (lc) Lennox Hearth Products. **F10** (tl) Reuters/Corbis. (b) Daniel Barillot/Masterfile. **F12** (bl) Stuart Westmorland/Stone/Getty Images. **F12–F13** (bkgd) Wei Yan/Masterfile. **F14** Harald Sund/The Image Bank/Getty Images. **F15** (tr) ©E.R. Degginger/Color Pic, Inc. (br) ©Phil Degginger/Color Pic, Inc. **F17** (tr) C Squared Studio/ Photodisc/Getty Images. **F18** (b) Michael & Patricia Fogden/Minden pictures. **F18–F19** (bkgd) Gunter Ziesler/Peter Arnold, Inc. **F20** Nasa. **F21** (tr) Gregory Scott/DK Images. **F23** Michael Newman/Photo Edit, Inc. **F24–F25** Michael Newman/Photo Edit, Inc. **F26** Steve Shott/DK images. **F27** (tr) David Young-Wolff/Photo Edit Inc. (b) Michael Newman/Photo Edit, Inc. **F28** (tl) Sciencephotos/Alamy images. (c) Philip Rostron/Masterfile. **F29** (br) CORBIS. (tbr) Getty Images. **F30** (l) Harald Sund/ The Image Bank/Getty Images. **F30** (c) Alchemy/Alamy Images. **F32–F33** (bkgd) JOn Eisberg / Taxi/Getty Images. **F33** (bc) Myrleen ferguson Cate/Photo Edit, Inc. **F34–F35** Blair Seitz/Photo Researchers Inc. **F38** (b0 ©E.R. Degginger/Color Pic Inc. (cr) ©E.R. Degginger//Color Pic Inc. **F39** (cr) Photofusion Picture Library/ Alamy Images. (tl) Jeff Greenberg/Photo Edit Inc. (tc) ©E.R. Degginger/ Color Pic Inc. **F40** (bl) Myrleen Ferguson Cate/Photo Edit, Inc. **F40–41** (bkgd) Joseph Sohm/ChomoSohm Inc./Corbis. **F42** (bl) Foodcollection/ Alamy images. (br) Tom Szuba/Masterfile. **F44** Alan & Linda Detrick/ Photo Researchers Inc. **F45** Ken Cavanagh/Photo Researchers Inc. **F48–F49** Greg Stott/Masterfile. **F54** (c) Foodcollection/Alamy images. (rc) Tom Szuba/Masterfile. **F56** Reuters/Corbis.

Assignment

A6, A7, A12, A13, ©Hmco/Richard Hutchings Photography. **A21, A30, 31, A38, A39, A44. A45,** ©Hmco/Ken Karp Photography. **A54, A55, A56, A57** ©Hmco/Richard Hutchings Photography. **A62, A63, A66,** ©Hmco/Ken Karp Photography. **A70** ©Hmco/Richard Hutchings Photography. **B6, B7** ©Hmco/Richard Hutchings Photography. **C12, B13** ©Hmco/Ken Karp Photography. **B14, B15 B26** ©Hmco/Richard Hutchings Photography. **B27** ©Hmco/Lawrence Migdale. **B32, B33** ©Hmco/Ken Karp Photography. **B40, B41,** ©Hmco/Richard Hutchings Photography. **C5** ©Hmco/Ken Karp Photography. **C6, C7, C12** ©Hmco/ Richard Hutchings Photography. **C18, C20** ©Hmco/Ken Karp Photography. **C22, C23** ©Hmco/Richard Hutchings Photography. **C24, C28. C31** ©Hmco/Ken Karp Photography. **C32, C33, C38, C39, C46, C47** ©Hmco/Richard Hutchings Photography. **C48, C50** ©Hmco/Ken Karp Photography. **C52** ©Hmco/Richard Hutchings Photography. **C45** (r) ©Hmco/Richard Hutchings Photography (lc) ©Hmco/Ken Karp Photography. **D7, D13, D20, D21,** ©Hmco/Ken Karp Photography. **D26, D27,** ©Hmco/Richard Hutchings Photography. **D32, D33, D43** ©Hmco/ Ken Karp Photography. **D44** ©Hmco/Richard Hutchings Photography. **D45, D49** ©Hmco/Ken Karp Photography. **D50** (c) ©Hmco/Richard Hutchings Photography, (b) ©Hmco/Ken Karp Photography. **D51** ©Hmco/Ken Karp Photography. **D56** (c) ©Hmco/Ken Karp Photography, (b) ©Hmco/Richard Hutchings Photography. **D57, D63, D65** ©Hmco/ Richard Hutchings Photography. **E5** ©Hmco/ken Karp Photography. **E6, E7,** ©HMCo/Richard Hutchings Photography. **E12** ©HMCo/Richard Hutchings PHotography, (bl) ©HMCo/Ken Karp Photography. **E13** ©HMCo/Richard Hutchings Photography. **E14, E15, E16** ©HMCo/Ken Karp Photography. **E18, E19, E20, E21** ©HMCo/Richard Hutchings Photography. **E24, E25** ©HMCo/Ken Karp Photography. **E26, E27** ©HMCo/Richard Hutchings Photography. **E28, E29** ©HMCo/Ken Karp Photography. **E36, E37,** ©HMCo/Richard Hutchings Photography. **E40** ©HMCo/Ken Karp Photography. **E42, E43,** ©HMCo/Richard Hutchings Photography. **E48** ©HMCo/Richard Hutchings Photography, (bl) ©Hmco/ Bud Endress Photography. **E48–E49** (bkgd) ©Hmco/Bud Endress Photography. **E50, E51** ©Hmco/Bud Endress Photography. **E52** ©HMCo/ Ken Karp Photography. **E53** ©HMCo/Richard Hutchings Photography. **F5** ©Hmco/Ken Karp Photography. **F6, F7** ©Hmco/Richard Hutchings Photography. **F9** ©Hmco/Lawrence Migdale. **F11** ©Hmco/Ken Karp Photography. **F12, F13** ©Hmco/Richard Hutchings Photography. **F15** ©Hmco/Ken Karp Photography. **F16** ©Hmco/Lawrence Migdale. **F18, F19** ©Hmco/Richard Hutchings Photography. **F21** ©Hmco/Lawrence Migdale. **F22** ©Hmco/Ken Karp Photography. **F24, F25, F29** ©Hmco/ Richard Hutchings Photography. **F30** ©Hmco/Ken Karp Photography. **F33** ©Hmco/Lawrence Migdale. **F34, F35, F40, F41** ©Hmco/Richard Hutchings Photography. **F46** ©Hmco/Ken Karp Photography. **F48, F49** ©Hmco/Richard Hutchings Photography. **F52** ©Hmco/Lawrence Migdale.

Illustration

A5, A22, A23 Pat Rossi Calkin. **B12–B13** John Berg. **B22** Terri Chicko. **B28–B29, B34–B3, B36–B37, B42–B43** Richard Cowdrey. B46 Terri Chicko. **C8–C9** Phil Wilson. **C18–C19, C20–21** Cheryl Mendenhall. **C25** Phil Wilson. **C44–C45** Bob Masheris. **C53** Robert Schuster. **D5, D16, D17** Promotion Studios. **D39** Steve McEntee. **D52–53, D54–D55, D59, D66–D67,** Bill Melvin. **D68** Patrick Gnan. **D69** Laura Ovresat. **D70** Bill Melvin. **E17** Promotion Studios. **E32, E54** Terri Chicko. **E56** Patrick Gnan. **F43** Mircea Catusanu. **F46–F47** Rob Hefferan.

Nature of Science

PHOTOGRAPHY: (kangaroo) © Martin Rugner/age Fotostock. **S1** © Digital Vision. **S2-3** © Tim Sloan/AFP/Getty. **S3** (r) Photo courtesy of the National Museum of the American Indian, Smithsonian Institution. **S4-5** © HMCo./Joel Benjamin Photography. **S6-7** © HMCo./Ed Imaging. **S8-9** © HMCo./Ed Imaging. **S10** Julie Dermody. **S11** © Issei Kato/Reuters/ Corbis. **S12** © HMCo./Joel Benjamin Photography. **S14** © HMCo./Joel Benjamin Photography. **S16** © HMCo./Richard Hutchings Photography.

Health and Fitness Handbook

ASSIGNMENT: **H12, H13,** © HMCo./Coppola Studios Inc. **H15, H17** © HMCCo./Joel Benjamin. ILLUSTRATION: **H12, H13,** Bart Vallecoccia. **H17** Linda Lee.

Science and Math Toolbox

H7 (t) John Giustina/Getty Images. (m) Georgette Douwma/Getty Images. (b) Giel/Getty Images. **H8** Photodisc/Getty Images.